AGEING

Report of the Social Policy Committee
of the Board for Social Responsibility

CHURCH HOUSE PUBLISHING
Church House, Great Smith Street, London SW1P 3NZ

ISBN 0 7151 6574 7
GS 940

Published 1990 for the General Synod Board for Social Responsibility
by Church House Publishing

Cover design by Iain Colquhoun

Printed in England by The Campfield Press, St Albans

CONTENTS

		Page
Foreword		vii
Members of the Working Party		viii
Acknowledgements		ix

Part I   INTRODUCING THE SUBJECT

Chapter 1   **Why a Report on Ageing?**   3

Approaches	5
Age and social policy	6
How the group worked	8
—consultation with the public	8
—consultation with political parties	9
The social and economic context of the Report	10
The religious context	12
Following in others' footsteps	12

Chapter 2   **The Facts of the Matter**   15

Population changes	15
Gender	18
Minority ethnic groups	18
Employment and education	19
Income and wealth	19
Social and health care	20
Marriage and divorce	20
Geographical variations	21
Housing and household composition	22
Outside Britain	22

Part II   SOME THEOLOGICAL REFLECTIONS

Chapter 3   **Ageing Observed and Experienced**   27

The contribution of the human sciences to Christian reflection on ageing	27
Our own experience of ageing	31

Chapter 4   **Christian Resources**   35

    The worshipping community   35
    Old Testament witnesses   36
    New Testament witnesses   38
    Jesus Christ   42

Chapter 5   **Faith and Ageing**   47

    The spiritual dimension in human life today:
        stages of faith   47
    The moral dimension of human life and ageing   50
    The wisdom to 'let go'   51

Part III   PROBLEMS AND POSSIBILITIES

Chapter 6   **Aspects of Ageing**   55

    Ageism   55
    Dependence and independence   58
    Ageing and the experience of black
        communities in Britain   60
    Risks and rights   62

Chapter 7   **Advancing Years: Some Possibilities**   65

    Expanding the horizons   65
        Reviewing life   65
        Staying well   67
        Continuing learning   69

    New relationships   70
        Grandparents   70
        Sexuality   71
        Friendships   73

    Participating in communities   74

Chapter 8   **Who cares? Who should care?**   76

    The experience of caring   79
    Women, men and care   82
    Attitudes to care   83
    Dementia   86

Part IV	ISSUES FOR THE NATION AND FOR THE CHURCH	
Chapter 9	**Public, Private and Personal**	97
	Changes in welfare	97
	Growth in the private sector of welfare provision	100
	The contribution of the voluntary sector	101
	Services for older people; income maintenance; housing; personal social services; health; education	103
	Guiding principles	112
Chapter 10	**Issues for the Church**	114
	Introduction	114
	The Local Church	114
	Deciding on priorities	114
	From generation to generation	116
	Caring for the carers	119
	Valuing the spiritual journey	120
	Rites of passage	122
	Death and heaven	123
	Using buildings creatively	124
	The Church's national role	125
	Challenging ageism	125
	Commenting on public policy	127
	Encouraging local policies and provision	128
	Training needs	129
	Improving employment practices	130
	Learning from religious communities	133
Chapter 11	**Summary of Findings**	136
Poem		141
References		142
Appendices		148
Further Reading and Resources		150
Organisations Concerned with Ageing		151

FOREWORD

To live is to age. From conception to death we are an ageing process. At first sight this may seem a melancholy thought, but the conclusions of this report are positive. Ageing is a fact of life which has to be recognised and then tackled in faith and hope. We may have to go through the 'terrible twos', the midlife crisis and the challenge of retirement, but the opportunities for fulfilling and enriching experience are great at every stage.

The Christian faith, set as it is within the offer and first fruits of eternal life, has much to say on these matters. In a secular materialist age, the Gospel is a precious gift offering a goal and an incentive to the way we approach each part of our lives. In the affluent West we now live longer, and we expect more than we have ever done, and yet we can still face the last quarter of our lives afraid of what is in store for us.

This report gathers together a great deal of useful experience and research and, at the same time as exploring the ageing process, suggests positive ways both as to how we can approach it ourselves, and how we can give the right support to others. It looks at society's attitudes to ageing—especially old age—and evaluates the social policies developing in this complex area of personal and collective responsibility. Finally it affirms what the Church is already doing in the life of congregations and institutions, and calls us to learn, to listen and to serve in a more informed and prayerful way.

Our thanks are due to Raymond Clarke and the working party who have brought together this rich resource and especially to Alison Webster who has written, revised, listened and revised again such a clear and helpful text. Margaret Jeffery offered substantial and much appreciated assistance in the later stages. Special thanks go to Deborah Cunningham and Pauline Druiff for their tireless work on the word processor.

I hope that at every level from house group to conference and synod as well as in families and in churches the report will inform, stimulate and encourage us all.

†JAMES STEPNEY

July 1990 — Chairman, Social Policy Committee

MEMBERS OF THE WORKING PARTY

Mr Raymond Clarke — (Chairman) Clerk to the Council of the National Council of Voluntary Child Care Organisations until February 1990; former Chairman of Age Concern Greater London.

Canon Michael Butler — Director of Chichester Board for Social Responsibility.

The Revd Vivienne Faull — Chaplain of Clare College, Cambridge. Member of General Synod.

Mrs Elizabeth Harbottle — Chairman, Christian Council on Ageing.

The Revd Dr Rupert Hoare — Principal, Westcott House Theological College, Cambridge.

Professor James McEwen — Professor of Community Medicine, University of Glasgow.

Mrs Sybil Phoenix — Founder Director of the Methodist Leadership Racism Awareness Workshop.

Professor Anthea Tinker — Professor of Social Gerontology and Director, Age Concern Institute of Gerontology, King's College, University of London.

Ms Alison Webster — (Secretary) Secretary of the Social Policy Committee.

ACKNOWLEDGEMENTS

We wish to acknowledge the many people who gave their time generously with expert advice or comments on drafts as our work progressed.

Particular thanks go to those who helped us in the early stages: to Professor Anthony Dyson who came to a residential meeting of the working party, and to Sally Greengross, Professor Malcolm Johnson and Dr Eric Midwinter, with each of whom we had most informative discussions. They are not, however, responsible for the way in which we may have made use of the advice which they kindly offered.

There is a study guide, entitled *Happy Birthday Anyway!*, to accompany this report which has been prepared by Joan King, Family Work Co-ordinator for Scripture Union. We are grateful to the Scripture Union for allowing her to assist us in this way. Further details of the guide are available from the Board for Social Responsibility, Church House, Great Smith Street, London SW1P 3NZ.

We are grateful to the Controller of Her Majesty's Stationery Office for permission to reproduce material from official reports. Detailed attributions are made both in the substance of the report and in the bibliography. We are also grateful to Jenny Joseph for permission to include her poem *Warning*.

Part I

INTRODUCING THE SUBJECT

Chapter 1

WHY A REPORT ON AGEING?

1.1   One way of starting to think about ageing is to visit your nearest card shop and look through the birthday cards. 'Roses are red, violets are blue. It's all right to be 50 . . . if you feel 22!' . . . 'Too old for spots. Too young for wrinkles. Happy Birthday!' . . . 'I can't believe that we're getting older. More experienced, better looking, more wonderful and valuable maybe . . . but older? NO! Happy Birthday anyway!'

1.2   Behind the jokes is a serious message. The birthday cards express uncertainty: is getting older something to celebrate or to regret? They also reflect a remarkable feature of modern society, that more of us are living longer. The age of 40 is increasingly promoted by the card industry as a turning point, the beginning perhaps of a 'mid-life crisis'. And it is common to find special cards for reaching the age of eighty, ninety and a hundred.

1.3   This report has been written to encourage discussion about ageing, to draw attention to the major trends and changes facing us and to explore particularly the role that churches can play. For although there is a growing body of research into many aspects of ageing, some areas have been relatively neglected. In particular little has been produced in this country from a church perspective.

1.4   A working party, set up by the Board for Social Responsibility through its Social Policy Committee, met between early 1988 and early 1990. It had the following terms of reference:

  i To consider the major issues of ageing as they affect British society today. This will involve focusing on the facts of the matter, social policy questions and theories about ageing.
  ii To offer a Christian contribution to the debate by reflecting critically and theologically on these trends, policies and theories, for example the meaning of independence and interdependence throughout the life cycle.
  iii To evaluate the Church's and wider Christian ministry in this field, paying particular attention to the contribution and needs of older people in the Church.

3

1.5   The working party represented a range of different interests and expertise. Unusually for a Church of England working party, half the group members were women and it was not chaired by a bishop.

1.6   The terms of reference make it clear that our brief was to look at the processes of growing old, not just old age. We were asked to reflect on ageing as it is experienced and understood through life and to explore the challenges it poses to the ministry and mission of the Church. We were also asked to pay particular attention to old age. Holding together an interest in the whole life cycle with a curiosity about the special value and needs of old age was sometimes hard. 'Ageing' as a subject potentially embraces the whole of human life and has no boundaries. Could any conclusions coming from such a broad study possibly have enough sharpness to be useful to the Church? On the other hand a narrow focus on old age is influenced by assumptions made about the ageing process in general, and some of the most interesting theological reflection is about continuity, maturity, fulfilment and relationships between generations.

1.7   The working party accepted this wide brief but was not uncritical of it. There were times when it was tempting to adopt a definite starting point and focus on life after, say, the age of 60. We were helped to resist this by the letters we received and by those with whom we talked. They were clear that old age can most fruitfully be seen in the context of the whole of life. So we decided to take the risk of breadth and to struggle with the tensions and paradoxes involved.

1.8   The other part of our brief which provoked much discussion was the role of theology. Should we try to integrate theological material into the whole report, weaving insights from the Scriptures and from Christian tradition into every chapter? Or was there a case for some sustained theological exploration, gathered into one section, which would inform the entire report but also stand apart? We chose the latter approach but have tried to make the connections with other chapters clear.

1.9   This tension makes the final report different from some other publications of the Board for Social Responsibility. Coming from the Board's Social Policy Committee it is right that there is an emphasis on the social policies needed to deal with a changing age structure, with new economic constraints and changing patterns of caring. It has also, however, seemed essential to address some of the psychological and spiritual tasks involved in ageing. Similarly it has been important to challenge the Church on its own prejudice towards elderly people—in short, its own ageism—and to look closely at the value it places on older people. Our conclusion is that much needs to be done to encourage a greater sensitivity to their contributions and needs.

Approaches

1.10   There are many ways of approaching ageing, and a wealth of literature on the subject. In general this report looks at ageing throughout the human life-span. However some necessary facts relating to chronological age are given in Chapter 2 because only then can the social and economic questions to do with housing, health care and social security be properly addressed. Throughout it is important to remember that chronological definitions of childhood, youth, adulthood and old age are bound by culture. As one submission to us put it, 'the time at which a person is classified as old varies in different societies; in developing countries people are regarded as old at a much earlier age than in industrialised societies. Using chronological age to signal the start of old age is a relatively modern development and has carried with it a related reduction in status.'[1]

1.11   Seeing ageing as a process has several advantages. First, it enables us to understand that the experience of being a child or an adolescent or an old person changes from generation to generation. A person in his or her 80s in 1990 has lived through two world wars, the creation of the welfare state, and a rapid rise in standards of living (though not necessarily his or her own). The 80-year-old man or woman in 2040 will have grown up with computers, television and generally higher standards of health care. Second, it puts relationships between the generations into perspective by emphasising that we all pass through stages. It becomes less possible to see people as belonging to distinct groups that have nothing to do with each other. Third, it allows a drawing together of the different strands of an individual's life, such as family, personality development, work, education and health.

1.12   Our approach to ageing was set out by the group at an early stage:

> We are interested in the way adults experience change and transition in their lives.

5

Ageing concerns:

> the passing of time and the gaining of personal experience
>
> discovering identity; comparison with peers and the sense of achievement or failure
>
> physical changes
>
> placing ourselves within a generation; understanding other generations, both younger and older
>
> shifts in dependence and independence—emotional, economic, physical
>
> discoveries about values and faith. How do I make sense of life?
>
> establishing and maintaining different kinds of relationships. Change and loss.

We are interested also in the way social and economic policies affect these human experiences, and in the part the Church plays.

Age and Social Policy

1.13 Dividing the population into age groups may not make much sense to the individual reflecting on his or her life, but there is no escaping them in the world of public policy. Many societies rely on age-related policies for the framing of legislation, the maintenance of law and order, and rationing resources. Without them collective administration would be impossible. Some of the most determined campaigns have been fought around issues of age, such as the nineteenth-century struggle to raise the age at which children were permitted to work in factories.

1.14 The criteria used to fix a particular age for a particular activity often seem arbitrary and occasionally bizarre. For example as a report from the Children's Legal Centre points out, in the United Kingdom a child can have a passport at six weeks, live in a brothel up to the age of four, drink alcohol in private at five, buy a pet animal at 14, own a shotgun, airgun and ammunition at 14, and marry with parents' consent at 16. It is legal to fly most aircraft, including helicopters, at 17, vote, own land, buy property, be tattooed, be hypnotised in a public performance at 18. At 21 a person can become a Member of Parliament or local councillor, sell alcohol, consent to a homosexual act in private with a man over 21, drive a heavy goods vehicle, and adopt a child. Under the Social Security Act 1986 some young people remain their parents' financial responsibility until they are 25, even if they are married.[2]

1.15   Later on in life there are some similar stages. Since 1940 the state retirement age has been set at 65 for men and 60 for women, though there are now several groups lobbying for the same state pension age for both men and women. Institutions have different policies for employees ceasing paid employment. Under the Ecclesiastical Offices (Age Limitation) Measure 1975 all male clergy instituted to a benefice from 1976 onwards must retire by the age of 70. In the Civil Service the age for both men and women is 60.

1.16   Age distinctions involve sensitive issues about the rights and duties of the individual and the role of the state. They frequently have financial implications on a large scale. Even quite small adjustments to the age at which an individual is eligible to receive a certain benefit can be extremely costly overall.

1.17   It is not only central government which relies on age distinctions. Most adoption agencies do not accept couples above a certain age as potential adopters of babies, and generally fix that point ten years or so before a woman's natural fertility ceases. Life insurance companies frequently have hidden criteria based on age about who is or is not 'worth' insuring.

1.18   Not surprisingly, therefore, it is usually when moral judgements and money are involved, that there is most debate. At what age is a girl mature enough to receive contraceptive advice and treatment without her parents knowing? (The limit is currently set at 16.) When should full benefit be paid to young people? (At present some do not receive it until they are 25.) What should the retirement age be and should it be the same for women and men? Is it right that a seriously mentally handicapped woman, up to the age of 18, can be sterilised on the consent of her parents? Who should give consent after the age of 18? How long should parents be expected by the state to bear some financial responsibility for their children?

1.19   There are similar debates about boundaries within the Church. When is a young person 'old enough' to be confirmed, or to receive communion? Should the Church as an employer follow the secular employment norms? When is someone 'too old' to offer themselves for the ordained ministry or for voluntary commitments such as becoming a Reader? How can church councils reflect a balanced mix of young and old people?

How the Group Worked

CONSULTATION WITH THE PUBLIC

1.20   Early on in the life of the group a press release was issued, which had good coverage in the church press and brought in many letters. They have been significant in influencing the working party's views and we are grateful to all who took the time and trouble to write. The letters were challenging and several have been quoted in the text.

1.21   Three themes arose again and again in the letters and will occur throughout this report. The first was a plea to take the *spiritual dimension of ageing* seriously. Several writers expressed the view that, important though it is for churches to be involved in practical caring projects for people of all age groups, this must be accompanied by a real attention to people's spiritual needs. Some older writers described a painful denial by others of their own interior journey. They said that younger people sometimes assume that the religious dimension—the sense of God's presence or absence, the desire to talk about what it means to be a Christian in the late twentieth century, the experience of doubt and certainty—simply comes to an end with the issuing of the free bus pass. In fact however many testified to a *growing* desire to reflect, to ask questions and to struggle with prayer.

1.22   One writer, commenting on the profound questions that in his experience arise for people in later life—questions about meaning and purpose and mortality and God—hoped the working party would assist those in a parochial setting to be better able to minister to the deeper needs of older people. He commented:

> Will the working party tackle questions about the development of spirituality in later life? Will it help us with the imaginative use of Scripture to stimulate and engage frail older people? Some quite exciting experiments are being made in this area as parochial clergy with a special interest struggle to be relevant to older people. Will it tackle the subject of prayer in later life and help us to explore how we can encourage older people in creative worship in residential homes and day centre settings? Will your working party give some guidance on the religious questions that older people carry in their hearts—if the Church has nothing to say about those questions, who has!?[3]

We have addressed the question of the training needed to meet these needs in Chapter 10.

1.23   The second theme concerned *ageism*. A distressing number of respondents had felt patronised or scorned purely on the grounds of their age. They said that clergy tended to apologise for them and assume that they were less interesting than younger people. One letter for example quoted the clergyman who, when asked what kind of a congregation he had, replied, 'I'm afraid they are mainly old ladies'. In other cases writers felt that the churches missed out on what older people had to offer, and that a potentially rich source of interdependence and mutuality was ignored. The letters made it plain that older people felt they had much to contribute. Again Chapter 10 looks at some of the ways in which the Church might address these issues.

1.24   The third concern was that *categorising people according to their age* is generally unhelpful. Many commented that they did not feel different at 70 from the way they had at 50, or indeed at 30, and yet all kinds of assumptions were made about them. They were critical of the way that old age is linked with the statutory retirement age, and therefore reflects a change of status from that of worker to non-worker. As one writer observed, 'the term "old person" covers a huge span, from age 65 to age 85 and beyond. We expect a great change in experience and attitudes over the 20-40 life span, so why do we expect stagnation later on?'[4] Much more important than arbitrary chronological distinctions, another writer argued, were life events—retiring from paid employment, becoming a grandparent, experiencing unexpected redundancy, or the death of a partner.

CONSULTATION WITH POLITICAL PARTIES

1.25   A second step the group took early on was to make contact with the political parties and to scrutinise their policy statements and party manifestos. Overall the party manifestos of 1987 were remarkable for their neglect of issues to do with ageing and old age. If they were mentioned at all, the focus tended to be on important but narrow policy options, such as the discussion about State Earnings Related Pensions or charges for eye and dental checks in old age. None of them showed much readiness to grasp the larger questions about changes affecting society. Correspondence with the Conservative Party led to a useful meeting with officials from the Department of Health. We were also grateful for discussion with senior members of the Labour Party and of the Social and Liberal Democrats. Our more detailed observations about public policy are contained in Chapter 9.

The Social and Economic Context of the Report

1.26   Major changes will affect the age structure of the population in the next 20 years. The main trends and their implications are discussed in Chapter 2. Although it is difficult to make comparisons, data available from the USA and Western European countries suggests that these changes are occurring throughout the industrialised world.

1.27   These demographic changes are accompanied in this country by important debates about the welfare state, about values and about individual and collective responsibility. New legislation like the Social Security Act 1986, and the National Health Service and Community Care Act 1990 focus attention on crucial developments affecting people of all ages.[5] There is an underlying discussion about the relative roles of the public, private and voluntary sectors, about how services should be delivered, and by whom. There is also a major debate about how much responsibility individuals and families should be expected to take in providing care. After the implementation of the Single European Act in 1992, British social and economic policies will be expected to relate more closely to those adopted by the European Community.

1.28   Earlier church reports have explored these general issues and the working party has drawn on them. *Faith in the City, Not Just for the Poor, Living Faith in the City* and the Methodist report *No Mean City*[6] look at poverty, welfare and interdependence. Church of England statements have emphasised the importance of welfare services being provided through central taxation. They have stressed that nearly all of us pass through stages when we are particularly vulnerable and in need of extra support. Chapters 6, 7, 8 and 9 look at these issues in greater detail.

1.29   Three further points need to be made about the context of the report. Sadly, the current political debate frequently relies on a distortion of language. The phrase 'dependency culture', for example, is nearly always used pejoratively. But there is a proper kind of dependence which is necessary for full humanity:

> The way the giving and receiving relationship is experienced changes as we pass through the different stages of our lives. It is important, however, to stress the reciprocal character of good relationships even in situations of dependence as with young children and their parents. Even very young children who rely on their parents for all basic care are nevertheless also contributors to the relationship.

The idea of interdependence opens the way for us to make a positive and creative use of the themes both of independence and dependence. Right at the heart of the Christian perspective on human life is the growth to maturity and responsible freedom of each individual person. There is a proper stress on individuality and independence. But there is also a clear acknowledgement that people must be open to receive from others.[7]

1.30   The second point concerns the current tendency to see ageing either as an overwhelmingly negative phenomenon, or one of unalloyed joy and serenity. We have not wanted to deny the pain and anger of some of the stages people pass through, or to gloss over the disadvantages experienced by some groups in society. But we have tried not to load arguments by using alarmist words like 'explosion' or 'burden' of old people.

1.31   Third, it is illuminating to consider how power relates to ageing. Some of the surprises and difficulties in life occur when those who have had power relinquish it. For example, being a carer of a dependent parent can involve a quite dramatic reversal of roles, the child becoming a kind of parent to his or her parent. Issues of power also commonly emerge in the relationship between parents and adolescent children. Helping a school leaver decide where to live, what kind of employment to seek, even what time to be in at night—all these involve delicate boundaries between the necessary autonomy of the young person and the proper authority of the parent. The use of the sanction of accommodation, money and opportunity can be a raw exercise of power.

1.32   The complexities of power within the parent/child relationship are seen in *King Lear*. Lear gives authority away by allocating parts of his kingdom. He expects to keep his status as father, but Goneril and Regan turn his material weakness against him and abuse him. Lear, unable to accept his powerlessness, then undergoes a further loss, the breakdown of his relationship with his daughters. He experiences a disintegration of personality and identity, and begs: 'O! let me not be mad, not mad, sweet heaven; Keep me in temper; I would not be mad!' (Act 1 Sc. IV). In our own generation research into how elderly people come to be emotionally and physically abused both by staff in residential settings and by their relatives shows how the perception of the older person as powerless can lead to their becoming the victim.

The Religious Context

1.33   That the working party received so much welcome and support is a sign that the churches are seen as having an important contribution to make. It is striking that in a country where only a small proportion of the population goes to church regularly, many people nevertheless use Christian resources at various points of their lives. Rites of passage continue to be widely sought. A third of all children are baptised in the Church of England, one-third of first marriages take place in the Church of England, and clergy are involved in the vast majority of funerals. Ageing is partly about moving through critical life events and the Church is present at many of these.

1.34   It was also plain that the Church was seen to have a role in questioning the economic and social policies of all political parties. Some respondents shared with us their unease that the late twentieth-century emphasis on materialism and consumerism, and the growing affluence for the majority in the industrialised world, is exacting a heavy price from rich and poor, old and young alike. Others expressed fear that one effect of this emphasis will be to drive a wedge between generations. They looked to the Church to watch over the values informing current political debate and technological advances.

1.35   We live in a pluralist society where different faith communities are strong and where Judaism, Islam and Hinduism and other faiths all have their contribution to make to an understanding of ageing. Our terms of reference make it clear however that the ministry and mission of the Christian Church should be our special concern. It seemed right to look at some of the current practice of the Church of England: Chapter 10 is devoted to this.

Following in Others' Footsteps

1.36   This report builds on work already done. Voluntary organisations like Age Concern, Help the Aged, the Centre for Policy on Ageing, Research into Ageing and the Family Policy Studies Centre, all produce an impressive range of practical and research material. In the last two years, several dioceses have started study groups on ageing and related matters; it has been helpful to consult with them. Bodies like the Christian Council on Ageing, the Church

Army and the Jubilee Centre have also produced studies, and magazines like the *Christian Action Journal* and *Christian* have devoted whole editions to the subject. Much more needs to be done; we hope that this report will serve as an encouragement.

1.37   It also needs to be said that some of the most perceptive reflection on ageing comes not from voluntary organisations and social scientists but from artists, poets, novelists and dramatists. Some examples are well known: Rembrandt's self-portraits in old age, Shakespeare's account of King Lear's bitter disappointment with his daughters, Philip Toynbee's diary of the last two years of his life.[8] Many of Philip Larkin's poems capture the ambivalence of middle age.[9] A fascinating account of how ageing has been seen in literature is found in Ronald Blythe's *The View in Winter*.[10]

1.38   This report inevitably has gaps. Ruthless decisions had to be made about boundaries, and some readers may come to the end puzzled by the omissions. For example we chose to write about dementia rather than depression in old age. A whole chapter could have been devoted to loneliness. However a study guide is being published at the same time and it is hoped that this will offer groups and individuals a way of taking up the issues raised, and pursuing areas of particular interest.[11]

Conclusion

1.39   Thinking about ageing is an intensely personal exercise. It is likely to arouse strong feelings. Our bodies grow and change, intimate relationships begin and end, loved people go away or die. We experience delight and pain. Thinking about ageing also demands an ability to connect this personal dimension with the social and economic background of the late twentieth century. It is urgent for the nature of changes already taking place to be understood so that wise decisions can be made about the distribution of resources and the provision of services over the next 30 years.[12]

1.40   What has become clear to us is that we are more likely to make those wise decisions if we are not afraid to face hard questions about life and death. It may be nearly impossible to view ageing positively and to value people from the beginning to the end of their lives if we are all the time in the grip of an unacknowledged fear of dying and death. Christians have no easy answers, but we do share certainty about

God's love and purpose for the world and all that is created. We do possess a sure hope of eternal life. Our tasks will be at many levels—allowing the presence of God to inform our understanding of our own lives, relating that understanding to the needs of others, and fearlessly scrutinising public policies in the light of our faith.

Chapter 2

THE FACTS OF THE MATTER

2.1   Part one of our terms of reference asked us to 'consider the major issues of ageing as they affect British society today' and to focus on 'the facts of the matter, social policy questions and theories on ageing'. Although predictions can never be made with certainty, major social trends can be described reasonably reliably. In a necessarily selective way this chapter sets these out and considers some of the implications.

2.2   The 'facts of the matter' about ageing are beginning to be better known. The press, television and radio are all giving ageing more attention. This is to be welcomed but also regarded with caution. For as well as the careful work being done by many research bodies there are also examples of statistics being used in an alarmist fashion. As was mentioned in the introduction, emotive phrases like 'the burden of elderly people' and 'the shortage of young people' merely blur complex issues of social and economic policy and reinforce the pervasive ageism that is described elsewhere in this report.

2.3   What follows needs to be read with an awareness that people's actual experiences are unique whatever their age. Assumptions made about people on the basis of their age group or generation may bear little relation to how a person feels about his or her age.

2.4   Statistical bases vary. In general the adjective 'elderly' is taken to refer to a man or a woman over the age of 65. Children are defined as the population aged under 16.

Population Changes

2.5   The population of the United Kingdom has grown steadily, increasing from 38.2 million in 1901 to 55.9 million in 1971.[1] Since then the overall total has remained fairly level, with only slight growth expected for the years up to the end of the century. There are now just over 56 million people in the United Kingdom. But the relative proportions of children and elderly people have altered considerably,

15

with a much higher proportion of people aged 65 and over. Figure 1 shows the shift that has occurred in the age structure of the population between the 1880s and the 1980s:

Figure 1. The changing age structure of the population

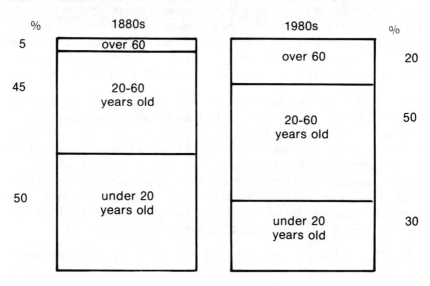

Based on Table 1.1 **Social Trends 17.** HMSO, 1987

2.6   In the United Kingdom there are over 10 million people of pensionable age—18 per cent of the population.[2] This represents a marked rise since the turn of the century, when the proportion was six per cent. The change reflects one of the great achievements of the twentieth century: the increasing life expectancy which improved sanitation, housing, nutrition and medical care have brought about. In 1981 for example, a new-born boy could expect to live to 70, and a girl to 76, whereas in 1906 their life expectancies were 48 and 52 respectively.[3]

2.7   The number of elderly people is increasing but not as dramatically as in the past. The change that will have the greatest influence will be the rise in both numbers and percentages of very elderly people. Much of the projected increase is due to a rise in births in the early years of this century. However people are also living longer. The growth in the numbers of people aged over 85 is particularly striking: as Figure 2 shows numbers will nearly double over the next 25 years.

Figure 2. The elderly population: past, present and future Great Britain

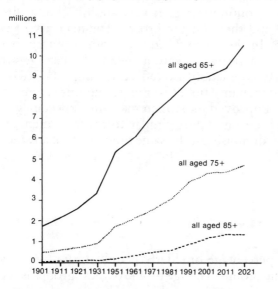

Source: *Population projections by the Government Actuary 1985-2025* OPCS PP2 No. 15 (HMSO 1987)

2.8   These changes in the age structure of the population are a challenge to those allocating resources and attempting both to meet present demands and to plan for the future. For voluntary organisations, including the churches, they serve as a reminder of the need to be ready to change.

2.9   For the first time ever, society has substantial numbers of people in the 'post-parenting' phases. Their children have left home, they may no longer be in paid employment, and there may be one, two or even three decades ahead of them. Increasingly there is the phenomenon of two generations of retired people; sometimes men and women in their 60s and 70s are still looking after their parents.[4]

Gender

2.10   Within these broad categories there are some important particular points. At birth boys outnumber girls very slightly, but as life goes on this is reversed and then the gap grows. The majority of elderly people are women. In the 75 to 84 group women outnumber men by almost 2 to 1, and in the over-85 group by 5 to 2.[5] The age structure of the present elderly population also reflects the impact of two world wars and the loss of men in action. Overall during this century female life expectancy has improved more than male life expectancy. As the lifestyles of women become more similar to those of men, so their life expectancy may diminish. At the same time, medical advances will help everyone.

Minority Ethnic Groups

2.11   A growing percentage of elderly people in the future will be from minority ethnic groups. The age profile of these groups is typically younger than that of the white population. There are also differences between groups which reflect different immigration patterns. Other than refugees and the parents of early migrants, most minority ethnic groups came to Britain in the early part of their working lives during the 1940s and 1950s. Most are therefore still well below retirement age, although over the next 20 to 30 years many more will reach this stage.[6]

2.12   The special needs of elderly members of minority ethnic groups will become more important over the next few decades as the population ages and its profile becomes similar to that of the white population. One implication for policy making is the urgency of making sure that health and welfare services are sensitive to the needs of these groups. Chapter 6 discusses this at greater length.

Employment and Education

2.13   Forecasts can also be made about the nature of work. The changing demographic structure is likely to affect the way that work is distributed between age groups. Concern is now being directed to the policy implications of a decline in the proportion of children and young people in the population. On the one hand there will be a smaller reservoir of future workers but on the other hand this may enhance the 'value' of older people who may be encouraged to stay in or take up new employment. Workplaces will also need to develop childcare policies which enable more women to return to work. Ideally employers should be supporting community-based childcare facilities. Continuing education (such as the University of the Third Age) is likely to become increasingly important, and Chapter 9 looks at this in more detail.

Income and Wealth

2.14   Older people have a growing economic independence. The rise of home ownership means that more older people have savings in the form of a home—indeed over 50 per cent of retired people now own their own home outright.[7] More people are retiring with the benefit of an occupational pension. A significant proportion of older people are therefore emerging as a group with economic and therefore political influence.

2.15   However despite an overall improvement in the economic position of older people, a considerable majority remain mainly dependent on state benefits. Retirement brings a sudden and dramatic fall in income, and for many represents the beginning of years of declining resources and living standards. Malcolm Wicks and Melanie Henwood comment that

> The position of people in old age reflects prior socio-economic position and social class, as well as sex and marital status. Inequalities which exist during the working life are perpetuated and amplified in retirement. Married couples are generally better off than the unmarried; men better off than women; younger elderly better off than the oldest; and spinsters better off than widows. This hierarchy reflects differentials in work experience and earnings earlier on.[8]

Social and Health Care

2.16   In general people remain in good health into their 70s. Over the age of 75 elderly people *are* likely to have some kind of physical disability but the extent of this is less than commonly believed. As Table 1 shows, over three-quarters of people aged over 85 are able to wash themselves all over alone and over 95 per cent can go to the toilet alone.

Table 1

Disability and Dependency			
%	65 +	75 +	85 +
unable to go out of doors	8.0	14.1	32.5
unable to get in/out of bed alone	1.9	3.2	6.3
totally bedfast	0.2	0.5	1.2
unable to go up/down stairs unaided	3.6	6.0	11.6
unable to bath/shower/wash all over alone	7.3	12.8	25.2
unable to go to the toilet alone	1.2	2.0	4.7

Source: 1985 *General Household Survey* findings reported in *Hansard* 15.3.88 col 552 and 21.4.88 col 546.

The popular image of old age as a time of inevitable sickness and physical disability affecting everyone is therefore far from the truth. Future generations of very elderly people may indeed be fitter than those in the past. The major illnesses of adulthood may be compressed into a relatively short space of time before death as the ageing process is slowed down by medical intervention.[9]

Marriage and Divorce

2.17   Although marriage itself remains popular, divorce rates continue to be high. One in three first marriages is likely to end in divorce, and one in two second marriages.

2.18   Divorce and remarriage change family relationships. Emotional bonds inevitably become more complex and challenging. There are also particular implications for caring. Traditionally the carer has been an unmarried daughter, but it is likely that there will be fewer of these able and willing to take on the major extra responsibility of caring for a dependent relative.

Geographical Variations

2.19 The elderly population is unevenly distributed around the country. Higher proportions of the resident population are elderly along the South Coast of England and in other traditional 'retirement' areas. Above average proportions are also to be found in inner city areas, particularly in the North and North-West of England. At the time of the 1981 Census the highest concentration of persons of pensionable age, 36.2 per cent, was recorded for the constituency of Bexhill and Battle. East Sussex overall is reputed to have the highest proportion of elderly persons in Europe. Figure 3 shows where the largest clusters of elderly people are.

Figure 3. Population of pensionable age at least 20%, local authority areas of England and Wales, 1985

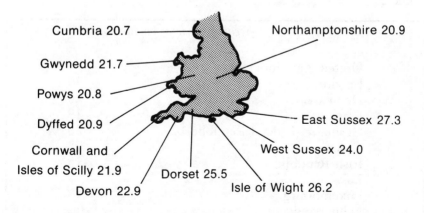

Cumbria 20.7

Gwynedd 21.7

Powys 20.8

Dyffed 20.9

Cornwall and Isles of Scilly 21.9

Devon 22.9

Dorset 25.5

Northamptonshire 20.9

East Sussex 27.3

West Sussex 24.0

Isle of Wight 26.2

Source: *OPCS Monitor* Mid-1985 population estimates for local government and health authority areas of England and Wales. PP1 86/2. May 1986

Housing and Household Composition

2.20   Approximately 95 per cent of people aged over 65 live in the community and not in institutional care. Indeed the proportion of elderly people living in residential care—four per cent—was the same in 1981 as at the turn of the century.[10]

2.21   In terms of household composition, the proportion of *all* people living alone has risen from four per cent in 1961 to ten per cent in 1985.[11] Part of the increase is due to more young people living on their own, but the most important factor has been the growth in numbers of elderly widows and widowers. Thirty per cent of elderly people aged over 65 in Great Britain lived alone in 1985.[12] Fifty-two per cent lived with a spouse, the majority of the rest with children.

Outside Britain

2.22   The demographic trends which have led to an ageing population in Britain are characteristic of the developed nations with a tendency towards lower birth rates and reduced mortality at all ages. Trends throughout Europe are broadly similar, although at 21 per cent the United Kingdom has the highest proportion in Europe of its population aged 60 or over.

Table 2

Persons over 60 as a percentage of total population in 1985	
	%
United Kingdom	21
Belgium	20
Denmark	20
France	19
Germany (Federal Republic)	20
Greece	18
Irish Republic	15
Italy	19
Luxembourg	18
Netherlands	17
Portugal	17
Spain	17
Source: *Social Trends* 18 HMSO 1988 Table 1.20	

2.23   In the European Community the number of people aged under 15 as a percentage of those aged 15 to 64 is expected to fall in most countries between 1985 and 2025, nearly halving in Ireland but remaining stable in the United Kingdom. The number of children in the European Community under 15 years, which fell from 72 million in 1965 to 64 million in 1985, is expected to decline to 49 million in the year 2025. The number of elderly persons (aged 65 or over) on the other hand, which amounted to 32 million in 1965 and to 43 million in 1985, is projected to have risen to 64 million by the year 2025.[13]

2.24   Similar points can be made on a global scale. The population of elderly people in the world is currently growing much faster than the population as a whole, and this is expected to continue far into the twenty-first century. The size of the global elderly population is increasing in both absolute and relative terms.

Conclusion

2.25   This chapter has looked briefly at the major changes which will affect our society in the next twenty years, and which will form the context for the individual ageing process. We are conscious that it is no more than a glimpse and that each section has had to be presented in a highly simplified form. The next three chapters move on to theological reflections on ageing, and to the resources of the Christian tradition.

Part II

SOME THEOLOGICAL REFLECTIONS

Chapter 3

AGEING OBSERVED AND EXPERIENCED

3.1   Creative theological reflection on the process of ageing needs to take account of objective observation and subjective experiences. A report such as this is likely to consist mostly of observation and to keep what it observes at arm's length. Yet to rely only on that would be a distortion, for the observers are themselves ageing. Subjective experiences, for instance of fear, of disorientation, of loss, of attempts at self-deception, of failing powers, are often painful, but they give the theme its importance, particularly for those who seek to hold on to the dignity and sanctity of the whole of human life. So this chapter will emphasise first-hand experience, recognising that this is hard to quantify because it is subjective, and that it is relative to our own culture, but not limited to it. One of the strengths of standing within the Christian tradition is that we find our own experience echoed and corroborated there, and partly at least we are shaped by it. But before we turn to that experience, we need to relate this chapter more closely to what preceded it.

The Contribution of the Human Sciences to Christian Reflection on Ageing

3.2   Chapter 2 used statistical material to describe and predict present and future trends. In doing this we were following the methods of the social sciences, which include a large element of observation. Such observation seeks to be as objective as possible, keeping 'value judgements' to a minimum. Whether they can be eliminated altogether is a moot point, for the very questions asked suggest a set of values that are important to us; and the language we use is also far from objectively neutral.

3.3   For example, to speak of growing older is not the same as to speak of ageing, as far as our culture is concerned. This working party was interested in both, but recognised that the 'feel' of the two ways

27

of speaking is different. You can measure growing older simply by the passing of the years. To ask the question 'How old are you?' is to hope for a straightforward answer, based on date of birth. That the actual answer may be a gloss on the truth, either by overstating or by understating the actual case depending upon the aspirations of the person concerned, is neither here nor there. We grow older as the years pass. We do not necessarily 'age' at the same pace. Indeed we can say of one another: 'It's years since I saw you, but you haven't aged one bit.' Or we might say of someone else, though we are very unlikely to say it to his or her face, 'They have aged a lot.'

3.4   On the whole, 'growing older' is less heavily laden with value judgements than 'ageing', and is more likely to be felt to be an experience from which one gains rather than loses. The process of ageing is felt by our society largely negatively. We try to retard it; we talk of it happening 'prematurely'; we deplore it when we see it in our friends. It is associated with loss of various kinds; it can be brought on by loss of one's job, by the experience of bereavement, by loss of friends, by the loss of the will to overcome setbacks or difficulties, as well as by physical and mental changes leading to some disability.

3.5   Ageing is thus a much broader term than growing old. It includes our feelings, our self-understanding, and our sense of our place in the world, as well as referring to physical and mental changes that are taking place within us. This report is about 'ageing' in that broader sense, though it asserts firmly the gains that come with ageing as well as being realistic about the losses. We thus want to correct the imbalance implied by our culture's use of the term, by pointing out and working for the good things that come with growing older.

3.6   Observation is often associated with the accurate recording of the passage of time. As regards our own age, however, as elsewhere, we can be 'economical with the truth'. We tend to round ages downwards; of someone who is forty-eight we might well say that he was in his mid-forties. The Old Testament writers, at least as far as their heroes were concerned, rounded ages upwards! By this can be seen the contrast between how we and they respectively view old age or 'length of days'—though when someone nears her century, we may well also round things upwards.

28

3.7   Studying the processes of ageing, however, yields more important knowledge than simply one's age. Human sciences describe and explain what ageing involves and therefore help us to make judgements from the point of view of Christian faith about the nature, values and priorities of human life. They help us see the purpose and nature of God who makes us as we are, and who declares that what has been made is good. There is also the rather different sort of observation of growing old or ageing offered by historians, writers, novelists, dramatists, poets and other artists. Here are glimpses into human relationships, histories, comedies and tragedies—referred to more extensively in Chapter 5 as the moral dimension of human life. We need to attend to their work as much as to the work of the scientists.

3.8   Some of the human sciences observe the individual; others study movements and changes at the level of a community or society, such as were outlined in Chapter 2. Examples of sciences which observe the individual are: anatomical, physiological and biochemical studies of changes to the human body, which can be seen as evidence of ageing; biological studies of changes to the human reproductive systems in males and females, and changes in sexual behaviour; psychological studies of changes in attitude, behaviour, mood, and feelings. Closely associated with these are medical studies which observe and diagnose disease patterns in the processes of ageing and then set about trying to correct them. Such medical work assumes the availability of finance and expertise and personnel to do the work, and reflects the values of particular societies and cultures. Surgery for varicose veins and for hip replacements shows the high priority our society places on mobility. Specialised work to remove facial wrinkles or markings is a sign of the desire to remain looking 'youthful'. Analysis is also done of people's 'needs', for example, for sleep, food, exercise, space and quiet. It is also possible to study changes in memory and intellect, and in the ability to deal with stress.

3.9   Such studies identify slow decreases in vitality and make us aware of our frailty. We are confronted with the need to accept and evaluate our mortality. We face the challenge to see how the various stages of life contribute to the whole. In this context gradual ageing must be seen as good, particularly when compared with its only alternative, namely sudden death, or sudden incapacitation through illness, accident or personal calamity.

3.10 Studies of human life seen as a whole include psychological studies of human growth and development, focusing on the emotional, physical, moral, and cognitive aspects of human being. These have recently been taken up and made fruitful for theology by James Fowler, writing as a theologian and psychologist, who has added a fifth aspect for consideration, namely development of a person's faith.[1] This will be considered in a later chapter,

3.11 Examples of the second sort of scientific observation of ageing, at the level of society are:

psychological and sociological studies of changing relationships, within the family, and particularly in relation to parent and child; changing roles, patterns of dependence, attitudes of people in a variety of relationships to each other; changing financial fortunes and relationships.

sociological studies of patterns of retirement from paid work; economic and psychological studies of the effects of retirement.

demographic studies of changes and movements in populations, relative numbers of different age groups in society; factors relating to minority groups in society (e.g., minority ethnic groups); factors relating to different treatment of men and women; the economic performance of different groups in society, their share in national assets and prosperity, in decision-making in society, their ability to contribute their gifts and experience.

3.12 Christian responses to studies in these areas are likely to be within the field of ethics. A key concept will be that of justice, and it will be necessary to look at different understandings of justice. For example, an understanding of justice which focuses on individual freedom and independence may be more appropriate in relation to people at the height of their economic wealth-creating potential (leaving for a moment on one side other considerations) than in their retirement. There are also acute questions of justice in respect of the more disadvantaged and marginalised members of society in their older age.

3.13 These questions lead to a deeper scrutiny of the values behind current thinking. For example much of the work of policy makers and scientists seems to rest on the assumption that there is such a thing as human progress, and that maximising human happiness is a primary goal. The nature of human happiness is often left undefined. It is simply assumed that all agree about it. But we might ask: does happiness always imply the attempt to remove or alleviate pain as far as possible? Is it to be found in the nurture and maintenance of as much independence as possible? How does happiness relate to truth? T. S. Eliot's comment in *The Four Quartets*, 'Human kind cannot bear very much reality', reflects this issue.[2] Do we work with a model of a particular period of life as the happiest?

3.14 Finally, in terms of our understanding of community, the response of faith will be likely to draw on the theme of *koinonia*— being members one of another, bearing one another's burdens, recognising that we are all strong and all weak in different ways. Again, fuller consideration will be given in Chapter 10 of this report.

Our Own Experience of Ageing

3.15 It would of course be wrong to divorce experience from observation completely. Awareness of our own ageing will enhance our powers of observation. We will spot things we would otherwise be unlikely to see. For this reason, too, experience takes priority over observation. But that does not mean we all need to be very old before we can say anything useful, for the experience of ageing begins quite young. Many adults in our culture were fascinated, when children, by the figure of Peter Pan. How often does a twenty-year-old not view her thirtieth birthday as a point of no return? And with the fortieth the so-called mid-life crisis is felt to set in (until you are fifty, at which point a forty-year-old is still a youngster).

3.16 This anxiety about the inexorable passing of time, and with it the inevitability of the process of ageing, may be a peculiar mark of our own culture. We are likely to look to people in their twenties, the beauty queen or the athlete, for models of the most perfect specimens of humanity. Our images of the perfect human relationship tend to centre on the young couple deeply in love with one another— and as yet without the cares of children. From that high point on, we can only go downwards. In this way, since our life expectancy has increased to a life span of 80 or 90 years, we have given ourselves plenty of scope for negative experiences of ageing: 60-odd years in which to deplore its happening.

3.17 In this report we want to argue strongly that such a negative view of ageing is one-sided and superficial. At the same time we recognise that it is a widespread view in our society, and also, at a more profound level, that there are indeed painful experiences involved in ageing and in accompanying one who is ageing, which have to be faced. We will refer to these again in this chapter and later in the report.

3.18   It is possible however to imagine seeing things differently. Suppose, for example, that our models of perfect humanity were to be found in the skilled craftworker, the artist who has perfected her work over many years, the person who has acquired wisdom through the exercise of responsibility, or patience and serenity through overcoming adversity. Again, should not a friendship that has been nurtured over forty years, or a marriage that has flourished over fifty, be highlighted and held aloft as the best possible examples of human existence?

3.19   What often happens, though, is that we become fascinated by the exercise of power. The wisdom that might be gained thereby is of much less value to us, as can be clearly seen by our sudden lack of interest in such a person as soon as power is relinquished. We no longer need to bother with them, and their wisdom is of no importance. It is responses such as these which make the transition to retirement such a painful experience of ageing in our culture.

3.20   It need not be so. In classical cultures, and in the world of the Old Testament, there is the respected figure of the wise old person, a model of the community's wisdom, stability, and blessing by God (such a person often found in the figure of the king). Perhaps a particularly good and poignant example of such a person is old Barzillai, who rejected the king's request that he should accompany him to Jerusalem, on the grounds that his age would make him a burden to the king and he ought to be allowed to return home.[3] Such a person is regarded as blessed by God and a source of blessing to the community.

3.21   The images or models we have of the best possible state of being human play a large part in our own experience of the processes and milestones of ageing. So much depends upon artists, novelists, and above all in our own society on the makers of films and television programmes, for the images of human beings held up for us to admire, imitate or ridicule.

3.22   Moreover the forces that favour short-term, fleeting expressions of human perfection over the patiently and arduously acquired qualities of life that come to maturity over a long time are very strong. The ability to innovate, readiness to change, adaptability, flexibility, these are the qualities that are felt to fit us for survival in a world changing as fast as ours is. And it is within this maelstrom of change that we have to discover and preserve our own identity, while at the same time coming to terms with the inescapable fact of our own ageing.

3.23   Take the first two decades of life. Apart from exceptional cases of accident or illness, in the first two decades of life human beings think of themselves as growing, not as ageing. Indeed they feel themselves to be 'growing up', first of all, then 'growing older', but certainly not ageing. Awareness of ageing seems to begin for most people in the third decade, and to become more acute as the decades pass.

3.24   Strong feelings about past, present and future are involved here. As we look at the past, we are likely to have some sadness that it is gone, a sadness that we may be exhorted to try to change into gratitude. We may seek to re-live the past, and find ourselves frustrated when we cannot do so. We may very well have to cope with guilt about what we have or have not done. We may wonder where all the time has gone, what we have actually done with it, what we have to show for it, why we were so busy that we never had time to savour what we were doing, or what was happening to us.

3.25   In the present, as the realisation of our ageing 'hits' us, we are faced with questions of identity: who am I now? To whom or where do I belong now? How do others look at me? Am I really one of those over-30s, over-40s, over-50s, over-60s? Well, I may be, in terms of years, but actually I'm pretty young and really get on best still with 20-year-olds. (Do they think that, though?) To 'feel one's age' presumably is to recognise the passing of the years and such recognition is commonly a matter of sadness.

3.26   Alongside the sense of loss and fear most people are also able to point to ways in which they are glad to be getting older. We may feel relief that a certain period of our life is over, that we have become stronger as individuals, less dependent perhaps on the approval of others, more certain of our own self-worth, more mature sexually and spiritually.

3.27   Looking to the future, there may well be fears, bordering on panic, as one realises how little time there is left. There may be unwillingness to face up to the future on the one hand, on the other a determination to plan it better, to make the most of it, to retain independence at all costs, to re-assess priorities. There comes the moment when secretly cherished ambitions are finally abandoned, and this may bring freedom. Is there also, mostly unspoken, a fear of death itself? Or is it rather a fear of the approach of death with its accompanying pain and accumulating disintegration? That would appear a commoner and deeper fear, in our culture, than that of future judgement before God.

3.28   All that is viewed from the standpoint of the personal experience of ageing. But for many of us it is seeing a loved one getting older which brings the reality of ageing home to us. This may be even more bewildering with the knowledge of our own ageing there in the background. But with a loved one in mind the questions will be: how can I continue to love him or her? I no longer see the person I knew. How can I cope with the changes going on in them? Can I speak about them, or am I to pretend things are as they always were? Do they see the changes themselves, or are they unaware of them?

3.29   This chapter has looked briefly at some of the contributions made by scientists to thinking about ageing and at ageing as it is experienced. Each reader of this report will inevitably bring his or her own life journey to this brief sketch. But for people of faith there is also a language and tradition which place the personal and collective journey through life in a wider framework. We turn now to some of the resources within the Christian community.

Chapter 4

CHRISTIAN RESOURCES

4.1   There are Christian resources which are relevant to the subject of ageing on which Christians can draw and to which they can point others. This chapter touches on four of them: the worshipping community, the Old and New Testaments and the figure of Christ himself.

The Worshipping Community

4.2   The first is the worshipping community to which Christians belong. Worship is at the heart of our life; it takes many varied forms; it may be formal or informal, liturgical or spontaneous. It binds people together, and at the same time lifts them out of themselves, enabling them to focus on the vision of God, within them, among them and beyond them. It is in that context that Christian identity is found, and the capacity to cope with change in oneself and in others is discovered. In pursuit of such identity, Christians draw on the tradition, make the Old and New Testaments their own, and seek to encounter Christ. Indeed they would say that they are led into worship by the Holy Spirit of God and are enabled to worship by Christ himself.

4.3   Of particular significance is eucharistic worship. Here Christian life finds its focus. Here (together with baptism) is the great celebration of God's creative work with individuals, families and communities. We are made anew, again and again, find our identity and know one another afresh, as we rediscover ourselves taken up into the story of the death and resurrection of the Son of God. Here the bewildering processes of ageing may be understood within the ongoing creative purposes of God. The experience of change we so fear is subsumed within the faith and hope of new creation in Christ. Here we are no longer alone, but members one of another. Our relative ages are no longer a matter of embarrassment or ridicule, but of celebration as we discover and enjoy a mutual interdependence, old and young together. At the same time, within that context of worship, our negative

35

experiences of ageing, and also of relationships between the generations, often fraught, sometimes downright impossible, can be held up for scrutiny, faced and even affirmed.

Old Testament Witnesses

4.4   Much of the experience of ageing, both negative and positive, can be found in the Bible, which plays an indispensable part within Christian worship. In the Old Testament the processes of ageing do not always lead to the figure of the aged person whose wisdom is respected like Barzillai, referred to in Chapter 3. For instance the prophet Isaiah (Isaiah 3:1-12) laments the fact that God has deprived his people of wise elders as leaders; he sees those who should accept leadership in their due turn refuse to do so. The Psalms too record negative experiences, such as Psalm 22, with its cry, 'My God, my God, why hast thou forsaken me?' In Psalm 71, the psalmist awaits old age with fear and anxiety lest it perpetuate present disaster and the apparent absence of God (which must be considered the greatest loss of all).

4.5   Nor does old age necessarily bring with it respect. There is ample documentation in the Old Testament of the tension, struggle, even battle that can sour relations between younger and older, both as individuals and as generations. A supreme example is found in the relations between Absalom and David, ending with the death of Absalom and David's bitter lament: 'O my son Absalom, my son, my son Absalom! Would that I had died instead of you, O Absalom, my son, my son!' (2 Samuel 18:33). One can see awareness of the potential difficulties between the generations in the very commandment to honour one's father and mother and in the exhortations to teach and care for the younger generation.

4.6   Nevertheless there is also in the Old Testament a strong belief that to come to a ripe old age, with a wisdom and a leadership respected and accepted by the community is how things ought to be. The Book of Exodus (Exodus 23:26) expresses the promise that God will 'fulfil the number of the Israelites' days', in the promised land. The promise is picked up in the prophecy recorded in Isaiah 65:20, which foretells the creation of a new heaven, a new earth and a 'Jerusalem for rejoicing', in which sin will not go unrequited and there will be no one who does not live out his or her days. But this is a promise for the future—

which belongs to God; it is not an account of how things are now. In the present age, according to the Hebrew Scriptures, there are two very different experiences of ageing and old age, one characterised by increasing debilitation and loss, the other by wisdom and respect in the community. We are not however left with an insoluble conflict between the two, but rather with the hope of their resolution in God's time. That is where the thrust of Old Testament experience points: in the direction of a time when there will be 'a new heaven and a new earth' and present pain, injustice and debilitation will be things of the past. Hope becomes the dominant mood; an expectancy for what God is yet to do, in God's good time. There will be a 'fulfilling of the days', a time when the lives of individuals and communities are brought to a wholeness, a completeness which is seldom experienced now. Such an orientation towards the future when blessing will far outweigh loss in old age must be a driving motivation for us in our response to negative aspects of ageing experienced now.

4.7 But it remains true in this present age, as Psalm 90 makes abundantly clear, that even if someone does come to three score years and ten, he or she does not necessarily look back on that long span of life as a fulfilled and completed whole. A thousand years are but as yesterday, so quickly time passes away. We may have seventy years of life, or, if we are strong, eighty, but even the best of them (if that is the meaning of the Hebrew: literally, their 'pride') are nothing but toil and trouble and are soon gone.

4.8 But characteristically the psalmist concludes by expressing the belief and hope that God will put things right, prefacing his prayer with the equally characteristic cry (Psalm 90:13): 'How long?' He then prays that the days of affliction they have experienced be balanced by an equal number of days of gladness, giving them a due reward for their labours, which up to now has been noticeably lacking. Other so-called psalms of lament (for example Psalm 37 with its determinedly optimistic view about the blessings the righteous inherit) make similar points, coming from similarly bitter experiences (see for instance Psalm 35). This expectation and sometimes even demand that things will be far better than they are now, is itself witness to the fact that the Bible does not give us a simplistically rosy or positive picture of ageing. If all were well now, no expectant hope for the future, based on the agonised cry of the present: 'How long, O Lord?' would have arisen. Why things are as they are, is of course another major theme of the

Old Testament, which would lead us into the story of the Fall, and to the Lord's words to Eve and then to Adam in Genesis 3:16-19: 'In the sweat of your face you shall eat bread till you return to the ground, for out of it you were taken; you are dust, and to dust you shall return.'

4.9 These psalms express the losses associated with ageing in general terms. There are, of course, particular groups of people who suffer more specific loss, for instance, widows and those who are without children. The plight of those who in their old age have no children to care for them, and of those who have lost their husbands, are singled out for special concern. Widows, in particular, are the concern of the Lord, and therefore of the community, as well as of their nearest surviving relative.

4.10 Here there seems a contrast between present ways of thinking and the biblical view. Our own thinking tends to be individualistic. If we ask about gains and losses incurred in the process of ageing, we have in mind the individual who is growing older. Such thinking needs to be subjected to the implied criticism of those whose lives are revealed in the pages of scripture. Certainly the psalmist bemoaned or enjoyed his or her own experience, but it was always seen in relation to others and to God. If he or she were blessed, then the community was blessed. If he or she suffered, then the community was involved as well. Above all, what was perceived as gained or lost in the course of life had to be understood in relation to the God of Israel. Sometimes God's ways were clearly understood, not least, when it came to loss, in terms of punishment, whether of Adam, or of the preceding generation, or of the individual. Sometimes God's ways were inscrutable. Sometimes, as we have seen in the psalms of lament, they were felt to be unjust. Sometimes what human beings experienced was deeply painful, and the harshest pain of all was the loss of the friendship of others and the apparent loss of the presence of God. And yet despite all this sense of loss, the abiding stance is one of hope, hope in the ultimate righteousness of God and the achievement by God of a wholeness of life for his people in which they would be richly blessed.

New Testament Witnesses

4.11 Many of these Old Testament themes are picked up and reiterated in the New. Older people are to be respected by the younger generation (1 Peter 5:5); widows are to receive particular care from the congregation (so long as they are genuine!); see 1 Timothy 5. And of course the early Church takes for granted the existence of an order of elders, alongside the apostles (Acts 14:23). Such an order is also to be seen in the model of the Jewish order of elders, referred to for instance in Acts 23:14.

4.12   There are however significantly new emphases within the New Testament, and new understandings of what have been referred to as the negative experiences of ageing. No longer are they simply contrasted with the hope for the future. Instead the negative aspects of experience (suffering, pain, hardship) are seen as signs that God's new creative work is being carried through to completion. In this sense they are themselves signs of hope.

4.13   The overwhelming experience of new life discovered through faith in Christ and within the Christian community itself shapes and directs the first Christians' understanding of the goal of their lives. For St Paul, to live is Christ and to die is gain (Philippians 1:21). The expectation of abundant life in the future, which will include life beyond death, fundamentally affects how life here and now is seen. 'My desire is to depart and be with Christ, for that is far better' (Philippians 1:23). This desire to be with Christ, in Christ's coming glory, turns the direction of St Paul's life (as he writes to the Philippian Christians from prison) so firmly towards the future that the question of the completion or wholeness of his earthly life pales into insignificance. Indeed his previous existence as a Jew now seems as loss to him. 'Whatever gain I had, I counted as loss for the sake of Christ' (Philippians 3:7). And yet he does anticipate further growth in this life: 'Not that I have already attained [the resurrection from the dead] or am already perfect: but I press on to make it my own, because Christ Jesus has made me his own' (Philippians 3:12-14).

4.14   A rather different emphasis appears in the Pastoral Epistles (the letters to Timothy and Titus). Either St Paul's earlier thinking has been modified in the course of time, or words are being ascribed to him by a successor who believes he can write in his name. This is shown especially by 2 Timothy 4:6-8 where the apostle looks forward to 'his departure', and can look back to a life coming to its rightful completion. He has fought the good fight, finished the race, kept the faith. He knows a crown of righteousness is laid up for him on the day of judgement.

4.15   Within St Paul's own thinking there is a further connection between the processes of ageing and the life of faith. This is most clearly visible in the second letter he wrote to the Corinthians. Here (in chapters 4 and 5) St Paul meditates on the fact that his outer nature is wasting away; in particular the tribulations of his work as an apostle are taking their toll, and he is afflicted in every way. Ageing is certainly taking place, but at the same time another process is also discernible: his inner nature is being renewed every day. God is creatively at work within him, and the losses he is experiencing in natural strength are counterbalanced by this new life within him. The two are inextricably linked. The processes of death and resurrection are interacting upon each other.

4.16   Here St Paul is not just balancing gains with losses, in coming to terms with the processes of ageing. He is so strongly aware of God's creative activity that he welcomes the losses as evidence of the gains that are taking place. It is through the processes of ageing and indeed of death, that new life and resurrection are to be found. On this view the losses are not losses at all. It is a moot point whether such a faith can be sustained in the less enthusiastic situation of a second or a subsequent generation of Christians, who still find themselves awaiting the decisive second coming of Christ and with it the resurrection from the dead. One would expect a revival of interest in the wholeness of human life as lived out here and now in this world, often in highly adverse conditions.

4.17   The New Testament writers explored another aspect of the subject of ageing: that of the maturity which is the goal of human existence as Christians know it in this life. The context of the community is crucial here; they were not concerned about the promotion of a maturity of the individual on his or her own. This maturity is something we grow into together, as the writer of the letter to the Ephesians emphasises: 'until we all [who the "all" is, whether Christians or all humanity, is left unclear] attain to the unity of the faith and of the knowledge of the Son of God, to mature manhood, to the measure of the stature of the fullness of Christ' (Ephesians 4:13).

4.18   The word which the Revised Standard Version translates by 'mature' means more literally 'perfect'. We need to reclaim this word, in its verbal and adjectival forms, to get to grips with the meaning of this theme. The 'maturity' that is sought is a 'perfection' of life that is to be seen in Christ, and found in the community of which he is the head. With such maturity we will no longer be children, tossed to and fro and carried about with every wind of doctrine (Ephesians 4:14), but will have grown up in every way into him who is the head, into Christ (Ephesians 15). Such growth is to be found in Christian life together, in which, paradoxically, it is our weakness rather than our strength that brings us towards 'maturity'. St Paul, writing about the thorn in the flesh that afflicted him, said: 'Three times I besought the Lord about this, that it should leave me; but he said to me, "My grace is sufficient for you, for my power is made perfect in weakness" ' (2 Corinthians 12:8, 9). Affliction, suffering, persecution, it is in the midst of these that we are made perfect, that is to say, reach maturity. 'Let steadfastness,' wrote St James (1:4) have its full (literally 'perfect') effect, that you may be perfect and complete, lacking in nothing.' It is, as we saw earlier, a process which St Paul knows to be not yet complete: 'Not that I am already perfect' (literally 'not that I have been already made perfect') (Philippians 3:12). It will be complete as we grow into the fullness of Christ, who prays that there will be a communion between his father, himself and his disciples, 'I in them, and thou in me, that they may become perfectly one' (literally 'that they may be perfected into one') (John 17:23).

4.19   To summarise, the Old Testament knows both the riches of growing old and old age, and also its tribulations. The two are juxtaposed, and both are seen within the hand and disposition of God, and in the context of community. We are not left with an unresolved balance between them; rather there is hope for the future in which God will restore and complete his creation—but not without judgement and the destruction of evil. In that state of things growing old will be a satisfaction, and old age a time of rightful influence and fulfilment.

4.20   In the New Testament the same elements are there, but the sense of impending change of the very nature of human existence in the near future colours and profoundly affects the first Christians' experience. Suffering is still present but not to be compared to the glory to come; indeed it is itself evidence of the new creation coming into being. The experience of ageing is at the same time the experience of new life. As Christians endure the present 'travail', so they come to maturity or perfection.

4.21   Such perfection or maturity the first Christians saw in Christ; in him these processes of new creation were already realised. So we must now turn to the way in which the first Christians saw Christ.

Jesus Christ

4.22   We have to be careful not to read the New Testament as if it would give us direct biographical evidence of Jesus' experiences of ageing. The purpose of the writers of the New Testament was to present Jesus of Nazareth as the Christ, the Son of God, the inaugurator of God's new Kingdom. Biographical detail is subordinated to this end. We can assume that Jesus grew up as a Jewish boy and young man in accordance with the Jewish customs and practices of the time. St Luke makes use of this background as he describes Jesus going to the Temple in Jerusalem at the age of twelve with his parents (Luke 2:41-52). But the purpose of this story is to show the special significance of Jesus' relation to his heavenly father, rather than to detail his experience of moving from boyhood to manhood.

4.23   The biographical details of Jesus' life are to a large degree hidden within the early Christians' faith in his ultimate significance in the purposes of God, part of which lies in the claim that it was precisely a human being who revealed himself to be the Christ of God. He 'suffered under Pontius Pilate'; he experienced the emotions of a human being; he was subject to the same sort of temptations; he went through the same stages of growth and maturation as other young men of his day; he was confronted with the same challenges of relationship with those around him. But we only get the occasional glimpses of these things, as it were by chance, as the story of how God was at work in him is unfolded by the Gospel writers. It is the writers of the apocryphal gospels who speculated about the details of his boyhood, thereby detracting from the main thrust of the story which was inexorably towards the events of the last week of his life in Jerusalem.

4.24   Up to that point we can make inferences about the stages of his life, and about those who must have shared his life. But such things as his learning a trade and working alongside Joseph pale into insignificance beside his baptism by John, his itinerant ministry of preaching and healing in Galilee, and his move towards a confrontation with the authorities in Jerusalem. The normal development of life is subsumed in the events that move to their dramatic conclusion in his trial and death under Pontius Pilate, at the age of about thirty-three.

4.25 Prior to those events in Jerusalem, the lifestyle which his public ministry entailed meant inevitably that the development of his life did not follow the normal pattern of a Jewish man of his time. He never married; he had nowhere to lay his head (Matthew 8:20); he clearly left his carpenter's profession, and took his followers away from their fishing. On one occasion his mother and brothers are reported to have lost touch with him and to be looking for him. When he is told of this, he appears to distance himself from them, as it were replacing his own family with those who do the will of God: 'Whoever does the will of God is my brother and sister and mother' (Mark 3:31-35). In this way a new community is heralded which transcends that composed of biological families. At the same time, he taught a very high doctrine of marriage. Nevertheless the coming Kingdom of God was the dominant motif of his teaching and while this by no means denied the importance of earthly natural ties, or the 'rites of passage' which mark change from one stage of life to another, it did call in question their inevitable primacy. It hinted at the creation of a new kind of community transcending familial, tribal, gender-based and racial distinctions.

4.26 Of course Jesus is not unique in having the normal passage of human growth and development interrupted and overtaken by historical events with a momentum of their own. Human lives are always an interplay between such growth and development and the events of history in which the particular life is played out. Indeed, if one is to ask an individual whether he or she has aged 'well', or 'prematurely', or 'badly', the question will be answered in relation to how they have coped with the historical events of which their lives are a part. An essential factor will be the quality of their relationships with those around them. Thus while ageing has to do with all those areas of life studied in the various social, physical and psychological sciences, it also has to do with the moral field within which personal life is lived. It is thus historical; and has to do with decisions taken, promises kept or broken, honesty, deception, the exercise and transfer of power, loyalty, guilt and feelings of guilt.

4.27 Whether people age well or badly will depend more on how they cope with the way others relate to them and how they feel they themselves have related to those near to them than on physical impairments that come with the passing of the years. One thinks of the effects of feelings of guilt (probably quite unjustified) can have on the lives of those who have cared over many years for an invalid relative.

4.28   It is in this world of changing relationships, religious and political movements, and historical events of which he was a part, that Jesus' life is played out. But for the Christian writers of the New Testament the events of this life are themselves a thousand times more significant because they are believed to contain within them the particular work of God.

4.29   Here was a life that came to a sudden and untimely end at the age of thirty-three. In relation to the life expectancy of those times such a lifespan would not have been considered as unusually short as we would consider it; nevertheless it came to a sudden and early end. The writers of the Gospels are not concerned with Jesus' physical or mental experiences of ageing prior to those forced on him in the last stages of his life. But they do speak of profound changes in his life-style as he arrived in Jerusalem for the last week of his life. W. H. Vanstone in *The Stature of Waiting* has shown how St Mark portrays his life moving from the active to the passive, with the decisive change coming at the moment of his betrayal (or 'being handed over').[1] Yet the Gospel writers do not portray a straightforward acceptance of passivity from that moment onwards. Their faith was that, even in his passion which involved a total loss of independence in the obvious sense (for he was a prisoner), there was a deep sense in which he remained in charge. This should give Christians cause to reflect on the experience of the loss of independence where it occurs for instance in the course of ageing. Had Christ not 'lost' his independence, would the world's salvation still have taken place? St Mark presents us with a Christ who brought about the world's salvation when 'reduced' (if 'reduced' is the right word) to dependence on what others would do to him and in passivity. The first Christians applied the words of Isaiah (53:7) to him: 'As a sheep led to the slaughter or a lamb before its shearers is dumb, so he opens not his mouth.'

4.30   Turning to Jesus' experience of God, one can see in the last stages of his life a deepening of that experience. His understanding of God as 'Abba', Father, has to stand the test of the agony he underwent in the garden of Gethsemane, and of death by crucifixion on Golgotha. It is here that one can see Jesus experiencing the most profound sense of loss as his life neared its end, namely loss of the presence of God, expressed in the cry of dereliction from the cross: 'My God, my God, why hast thou forsaken me?'—a quotation from Psalm 22 already referred to. And yet this experience of loss would come to be regarded by his followers as an essential motif in his vision of the love of God. For the rest of us that cry remains an incomparable gain.

4.31 The New Testament writers are able to look at Jesus' life as a whole, moving towards its inevitable climax at the time of his death outside Jerusalem. It is to be seen as a perfecting of love, a maturation of his whole being, to use the language of maturity to which reference has already been made. It is entirely appropriate that St John (19:30) records Jesus' last words as: 'It is finished' or 'completed'. The word is the verbal form of that which was translated by 'mature' in the Ephesians passage. St Paul sees Jesus' life and death as the perfect example of obedience (Romans 5:18-21); the letter to the Hebrews sees them as the perfect sacrifice (7:26, 27). Thus the New Testament does not see his life as cut short, but as complete, and in so doing it puts a question mark against the desire for 'length of days' as a necessity for human life.

4.32 The Lukan account of the last words of Jesus from the cross (Luke 23:46) are also relevant to our theme: 'Father, into thy hands I commend my spirit.' Here is an example of 'letting go', which is not only appropriate (if exceptionally hard) in the extreme circumstances of death by crucifixion, but which as an expression of trust can be seen as part and parcel of the life of faith. As the author of the letter to the Hebrews puts it: 'We are to look to Jesus the pioneer and perfecter of the faith, who for the joy that was set before him endured the cross, despising the shame, and is seated at the right hand of the throne of God' (Hebrews 12:2). Such a 'letting go' is not a passive resignation in the face of the inevitable, but a readiness to trust God and to trust others in such a way as to let go of the attitude that seeks at all costs to retain independence. A loss of independence can confer the gain of the companionship and help of others. When we stop trying to initiate and control, we may find a mutuality in shared humanity which had previously eluded us.

4.33 Such a giving up of control also means relinquishing power. There are many different ways in which the first Christians saw Christ's death and resurrection as a handing on of his power to them. The words he spoke to his disciples at his last meal with them: 'This is my body, this is my blood, for you,' imply the transfer of his life to them, but only through his own death. His washing of their feet, at that same meal, and his breathing on them after his resurrection, are both ways of expressing the transfer of his power and life to them. 'As the Father sent me, so I send you' are the words recorded of him in John 20:21.

4.34   Finally it is important to remember those who accompanied Jesus during his last days. There were of course the disciples who tried to stay with him, but who eventually 'all forsook him and fled'. There were also the women who St Mark records as 'looking on from afar' after the others had run away (Mark 15:40). These were the women who had ministered to him (15:41); his 'carers', to use the modern idiom, remained with him through the last days of his life and looked after his body after his death. There was the woman who anointed him in the house of Simon at Bethany; there was his mother; and there were the other women who were with Joseph of Arimathea, as he laid his body in the tomb. And it was three of these women who first came face to face with his resurrection.

Chapter 5

FAITH AND AGEING

The Spiritual Dimension in Human Life Today: Stages of Faith

5.1   Most people acknowledge that a spiritual dimension is part of their life. We may not know what it is exactly and very often it may not be expressed in traditional religious terms, but we recognise spirituality in ourselves and in others. By 'spirituality' we generally mean those beliefs, hopes or ideals which give purpose to life over and above our physical progress or our social achievements. Spirituality holds together the emotions, convictions and attitudes that characterise an individual's life history. It is this interior part of us that is most keenly exercised when we think about the purpose of our life, our future or our destiny.

5.2   Spirituality is expressed not only in individual terms: it may also be experienced within the life of a family or a community. Spirituality is subjective; it is what people live by, and it helps them to look forward. For Christians these experiences will often also be linked with prayer, worship and personal devotional discipline.

5.3   Spiritual awareness can develop in childhood, perhaps through observing, in wonder, the miracles of the natural world. In *Memories, Dreams, Reflections,* Jung describes two early memories:

> One memory comes up which is perhaps the earliest of my life, and is indeed only a rather hazy impression. I am lying in a pram, in the shadow of a tree. It is a fine, warm summer day, the sky blue, and golden sunlight darting through green leaves. The hood of the pram has been left up. I have just awakened to the glorious beauty of the day, and have a sense of indescribable well–being. I see the sun glittering through the leaves and blossoms of the bushes. Everything is wholly wonderful, colourful, and splendid.

> Another memory: I am sitting in our dining-room, on the west side of the house, perched in a high chair and spooning up warm milk with bits of broken bread in it. The milk has a pleasant taste and a characteristic

smell. This was the first time I became aware of the smell of milk. It was the moment when, so to speak, I became conscious of smelling. This memory, too, goes very far back.[1]

5.4 Spiritual needs may be acutely felt as part of the process of adolescence. In mature adult life many events create a sense of growth and change. Although not always recognised or expressed as such, there is a spiritual component to human love and within many patterns of human relationship. Spirituality unites the physical, mental and emotional strands of our lives into that wholeness which is our created being. A sense of elation may derive from spiritual experience. We can be so inspired as to be drawn to God, or to experience a revelation about the purpose, and end, of our being.

5.5 The spiritual dimension in our lives changes as we move into our middle and later years. Some experiences or conditions can lead to a loss of spirit and others may give us a great sense of fulfilment. At any stage a person can lose the awareness of being of any value or become aware of having little to contribute to life. A sense of significance, progress or growth may be diminished or lost because of doubts that life scarcely makes sense.

5.6 The spiritual needs of older people are fundamentally the same as those of other age groups. Yet they may differ in scale and character because of changes or losses which accumulate and, possibly, accelerate in later life. There may be a kind of interior distress due to the difficulty of adjusting to what is happening. The crises which come to everyone who lives a long life are not easily faced in a creative way, either by the person concerned or by relatives, friends, counsellors or pastors.

5.7 Chapter 3 sketched out briefly the contribution of the social sciences to our understanding of the processes of ageing; here scientific observation was to the fore, personal experience in the background. Amongst the sciences reference was made to the study of human growth and development and within that to Fowler's work on faith development.[2] Fowler marked out six stages of faith which human beings may experience in their journey through life. For his purposes faith may or may not be theistic; it refers to people's ways of seeing their lives and the world around them, how they relate to authority, understand ritual and symbol, and participate in a wider group or community. He divided the whole life-span into seven eras: infancy, early childhood, childhood, adolescence, young adulthood, adulthood and maturity (60 +). Within this framework he sees six ways of having faith, which he terms intuitive-projective faith (early childhood), mythic-literal faith (school years), synthetic-conventional faith (adolescence), individuative-reflective faith (young adulthood), imaginative faith (mid-life and beyond), and finally universalising faith. These were described in the Board of Education's report *Children in the Way* (NS/CHP, 1988). The relevant extract is contained in Appendix B.

5.8   We recognise the importance of Fowler's attempt to delineate phases of faith, to some extent at least reflecting different stages of life. Those seeking to care for others at the different stages of their lives, and particularly in periods of transition, need to be aware that they may or may not have moved on, in terms of their faith, to a maturity commensurate with their age. Many may have been held back to a way of having faith which belonged to an earlier stage of their lives, and may need help in moving on.

5.9   On the other hand, several words of caution are in order. There is no requirement that one 'moves on': indeed at certain stages of life, one may move 'back'; some may live their lives perfectly successfully and happily at what would appear a less mature or sophisticated level than Fowler's progressive scheme might suggest.

5.10   Moreover the model gives prominence to the psychological understanding of the individual. This can lead to the individual being seen in isolation from his or her function in society, and from the actual 'give and take' of human lives in their historical and moral setting. The Old Testament theologian Walter Brueggemann gives a very useful corrective to this in *Hope Within History*.[3] He shows how for the Jews, fed primarily on the Hebrew Scriptures, development of faith is found in the recognition of their oppression, the articulation of the pain they experience, and the discovery of a hope that God will make things different. This is a community-centred approach to faith, nurtured in a shared experience of worship and of life, and implicitly subversive of the established order. We can see its counterpart in the Christian experience of the eucharistic worship of the community.

5.11   Above all Brueggemann argues that the Bible tends to concentrate on the moments of change in a person's or a people's life rather than on the relatively static stage they may have reached. Our own approach in this report, which concentrates on ageing rather than one particular stage of life, is in line with this. To concentrate on ageing is to affirm the transitional stages of life as good in themselves, and as leading to life and new birth (one is reminded of the use in the Bible of the image of the woman in labour). Our Christian stance must be one of hope, hope that change, however traumatic, is in the hand of God, and is essentially to do with resurrection and new life, rather than with deterioration and decay.

5.12   Nevertheless, those who seek to enable themselves or others to cope with such changes may be helped by asking at what stage of faith they are, and whether their faith is encouraging or hindering them in coping with the demands of the moral dimensions of their lives. Fowler has done us a service by pointing out that the structure of faith, *how* we believe, changes with the various stages of life.

The Moral Dimensions of Human Life and Ageing

5.13   Chapter 3 sought to explore our subjective experiences of ageing. Chapter 4 identified certain Christian resources as relevant to these experiences. In the course of outlining them, our attention was drawn to the 'moral dimensions' in human life, those good or bad experiences which affect deeply the ways in which people grow older and move towards their deaths. In particular, consideration of the life of Christ led us to take account of how people treat each other. The point is a simple one; it is that personal and social ethics are centrally relevant to how people age. At the level of personal ethics, the degree to which people experience friendship, loyalty, love, treachery, violence, insensitivity, for example, will enhance or diminish their lives. At the level of social ethics, justice or injustice, poverty or wealth, disease or malnutrition, respect or exploitation, will all play their part in how people grow older and come to die. At both social and personal levels, how guilt and guilt feelings are handled, how repentance and forgiveness are experienced, are all very much to the point.

5.14   In terms of these 'moral dimensions', Christian experience of life which is centred on worship, and specifically on eucharistic worship, is directly relevant. Here guilt, repentance and forgiveness are all regular experiences of the participants. In the eucharist a vision of personal and social relationships is given us which should enable us to see and to tackle issues of justice that present themselves in the life of society around us. At the same time, because the emphasis in the eucharist is always on thanksgiving for the work that God through Christ has done for us, rather than on anything we may be or do ourselves, a sense of proportion is given to our activity, and our innate activism is balanced by contemplation and worship.

5.15   We have to hold in balance our rightful sense of responsibility in caring for others, and attempting to right society's injustices, with a vision of God who is beyond us and in the worship of whom we find our true rest. Indeed such an attitude of contemplation will rid our active engagement with the world's problems of the self-concern that otherwise bedevils such engagement. It is moreover an attitude of mind and spirit which is appropriate to the experience of ageing. Central to it is hope, an expectant waiting on God, and a readiness to accept dependence on others when it comes. It is an attitude of deep prayerfulness, directed upon the vision of God.

The Wisdom to 'Let Go'

5.16   It is in this context that we are to look for the wisdom that cultures other than ours have frequently associated with the old person. Such a wisdom is not only appropriate for the aged person, but for all of us as we age, and is a gift which the older person can offer to those younger people around them as they dash about in their hectic over-busyness. It can be a real life-saver.

5.17   Such wisdom has to do with 'letting go', and with learning not to hold on to the past. It involves getting the balance right between retaining independence and an active initiatory style of life on the one hand and accepting increasing dependence, which rejoices in the help and companionship others often want to give. Such a wisdom will have a sense of proportion and humour about personal ambition, an appreciation of what can be changed, and what cannot. On the other hand it will not amount to resignation, or apathy, or ceasing from 'looking for the coming of the Kingdom', as one of our eucharistic prayers puts it. As St Peter says, quoting the prophet Joel in Acts 2: 'the Spirit of God is to be poured out on all flesh, so that they prophesy; the young will see visions, and the old will dream dreams'.

5.18   At the same time such a wisdom will attempt to see life as a whole, a whole which should be offered back to God. It will see God as the Creator who continues his creative work in us right through our lives, to the point of death and beyond. Robert Browning expresses this in the opening lines of his poem, *Rabbi Ben Ezra:*

> Grow old along with me
> The best is yet to be,
> The last of life, for which the first was made
> Our times are in his hand. . .

Later in the same poem he affirms:

> Maker, remake, complete,
> I trust what Thou shalt do.

5.19   However, with that positive and trusting attitude in mind, we cannot avoid recognition of the baffling problem of evil, suffering and pain, sudden death, crippling disease, which can shatter any picture of the wholeness of life for so many, and which can be so painfully present in the experience of ageing.[4] At the same time we are encouraged to see diminishment and the decrease of power, to the point of death, as necessary for the birth of something new. One living thing dies, to give place to another: here is an elemental process within the universe, hallowed for us and brought into focus by the death of Christ.

5.20 Such a view of ageing and old age runs contrary to much practice and ideology on the subject. On the one hand, attuned to our present culture's ideology of independence of the individual and liberation from the 'nanny state', is a common current philosophy that elderly people should maintain their independence at almost all costs, and for as long as possible. On the other hand, what people may experience in old age is a sense of debilitating dependence and passivity following the traumatic move from productivity to a non-productive life style at the point of retirement.

5.21   The Christian picture of a mature and balanced human life contains elements of independence and dependence. All of us need the opportunities and the means to give, and all of us need to discover the liberty of being able to receive. Giving and receiving vary as we pass through different stages of our lives. Even very dependent people may be able to give by offering love and by affirming those people who care for them. To deny such possibilities is to devalue much of human experience.

Part III

PROBLEMS AND POSSIBILITIES

Chapter 6

ASPECTS OF AGEING

6.1   So far we have looked at some of the trends which will affect society in the next decades, and which influence the context within which the individual ageing process occurs. We have also examined biblical material and explored the resources which Christians can draw on when reflecting upon ageing.

6.2   Ageing, this report suggests, concerns the whole lifespan. It is about a process from birth to death which involves us in certain stages and changes. Two cautionary notes have been sounded from the beginning. First, an exclusive focus on one ageband is too limited. A close look at, say, adolescence or old age is sometimes necessary, particularly for the planning of services and the rationing of resources. But in general such an approach gives a false impression of discrete differences between age-bands and tends to emphasise separateness and discontinuity rather than commonality and continuity. Second, an approach which relies too heavily on generalisations is likely to lead to distortion. What happens to the individual is profoundly affected by race and gender, socio-economic position and family context.

6.3   It is now time to present four aspects of ageing that recurred frequently in our discussions: ageism, dependence and independence, the experience of the black community, and risks and rights. The aim is not to explore each extensively but to indicate matters of special concern. In the next chapter we gather some of the most positive dimensions of ageing.

Ageism

6.4   A new word has entered the English language in the last twenty years—ageism. Ageism involves discrimination against people on the basis of age; it 'deprives people of power and influence'[1] and is based on 'fear and folklore'.[2] It affects young people as well as old. And, as Franklin and Franklin have pointed out: 'Ageism involves a cruel irony. White racists never become black and male chauvinists do not become women, but those who hold ageist views must necessarily grow old and by so doing, fall victim to their own prejudices.'[3]

6.5   The word may be new and perhaps uncomfortable to some but the phenomenon is not. Chapter 4 showed how the Old and New Testaments, while reflecting positive attitudes to ageing, contain cries of despair and sorrow at the process of growing old. There is celebration of old age in literature and visual art, but also fear, and many examples of old people being ignored and scorned.

6.6   It is important to address these negative attitudes to ageing. Ageism affects the way in which older people see themselves, are perceived by others and the way that provision for them has developed. This section looks at how ageism operates; Chapter 10 picks up the theme in relation to the Church.

6.7   A preliminary point must be made about women. Ageism reinforces sexism in a number of ways. First, women substantially outnumber men among elderly people. Second, the ageing process is unequal in its treatment of the sexes. To quote Franklin and Franklin again:

> Society tends to value men for their intellectual abilities, their experience, but especially for occupational and careeer achievements which tend to develop with age. Even their physical appearance can be considerd enhanced by age, with greying hair and wrinkles being perceived as conveying 'maturity'. Women however are valued more for their physical beauty (often measured directly by youth), their sexuality and their capacity to reproduce, which are each undermined by age. One stereotype of women defines them as carers, nurturers, wives and mothers and when old women are unable to contribute to society through any of these assigned roles they are deemed obsolete. . . . Ageing may flatter men but nearly always threatens women. Advertisements, especially those for cosmetics, play on women's desire for youth by offering them wish-fulfilment fantasies in which they are mistaken for their daughters; it is doubtful whether fathers would be happy to be mistaken for their sons.[4]

6.8   A disturbing feature of ageism is that so much of it is based on fiction. The Search Project *Against Ageism* has identified a number of myths surrounding old age,[5] namely the myths of chronology (that old age is defined by years lived), ill health, senility and mental deterioration, inflexible personalities, isolation, misery and unproductivity.

6.9   However, these features of life apply to only a small proportion of the elderly population. Old age is *not* necessarily a time of sickness and disability. For example, only five per cent of people over the age of 75 are likely to suffer from senile dementia. Table 1 in Chapter 2 shows that three-quarters of people aged over 85 can wash all over alone. Over 80 per cent of elderly people maintain independent households. As Chapter 7 suggests, the positive aspects of being old are many—greater freedom, the possibility of strong relationships with adult children and grandchildren, continuing friendships, continuing sexual vitality.

6.10   Prejudices against old people are apparent in everyday language and colloquial expression and in their portrayal in the media. Phrases like 'silly old biddy', 'he's a real old woman' reflect feelings of scorn and separateness. Research into how elderly people are presented in the media is revealing some fascinating distortions. Many television programmes for example misrepresent the percentage of older people in the population. In an American study of 'prime time' TV drama, which monitored 1365 programmes over a ten-year period, under three per cent of characters were aged over 65, compared to 11 per cent of the actual population. Similarly advertisements tend to feature a disproportionate number of younger people. Old people are also very often portrayed as figures of fun. Dot, Ethel and Lou in *EastEnders,* Old Steptoe in *Steptoe and Son*, and the men in *Last of the Summer Wine* include a variety of stereotypes of old people as domineering, pathetic, unbalanced.

6.11   Negative images of old people presented by the media have two important effects. They influence the way in which old people are treated by the general public as well as by some members of the caring professions. The images also influence older people's perception of themselves and undermine their morale.

6.12   There is however encouraging evidence of change. Some of the push for this is coming from old people themselves. Although there is as yet no United Kingdom equivalent of the Gray Panthers (a campaigning organisation of older people in the USA), there are now groups of older people who are showing a new assertiveness. They are beginning to question the assumptions behind services for elderly people, not least the rigidity that has marked the demarcation between work and retirement. Campaigns to end age discrimination in employment, to raise pension levels, to maintain and improve adult education, are all beginning to flourish.

6.13   Another trend which may influence attitudes for the better is likely to be the growing economic prosperity of some elderly people, and their new attractiveness to the commercial sector. Elderly people's potential as the 'new consumers' has not been lost; the over-50s have been described as 'the splurge generation', 'the untapped market', and there are numerous puns on grey hair, such as 'The Grey Market—a golden opportunity', and The Gold among the Grey'.[6] Advertising and marketing agencies have recognised their potential for the holiday, leisure and insurance industries.

6.14   The Christian tradition offers a way of understanding ageing that is basically affirmative. A knowledge that each person is made in the image of God, created for life in community with others and with God, means that every person is to be valued. Economic status, the capacity to produce and consume, and social standing are not ultimately of the greatest importance. The detailed practical implications of these values have to be worked out in the complex world of economic and social policy, but one consequence is clear: that each person matters uniquely means that his or her life must be valued and honoured, no matter how old or frail.

6.15   Christians therefore ought to be among those—including those of other faiths and none—who challenge contemporary attitudes. They can affirm God's presence throughout life, and throughout diminishment as well as growth. They may be able to show the significance of so-called failure as well as so-called success. Further attention to this—including the Church's own ageism—is given in Chapter 10.

Dependence and Independence

6.16   One way of looking at ageing is to see it as a process of moving through periods of dependence and independence. There are certain stages which almost everyone experiences. The vulnerability of the infant is replaced by a growing autonomy in the older child. The child starts school, moves eventually into adolescence, and probably from there to paid employment. Most people form a long-term central relationship with another adult in their teens or twenties, and experience having children, and caring for older relatives. A significant minority at any one time may be single and may also have responsibility for children or frail relatives. Many old people remain fit and healthy; but some towards the very end of life will require the constant reliable care that they needed as young children.

6.17 'Dependence' and 'independence' have become loaded words, 'dependence' being seen as a bad thing, and 'independence' a virtue. The phrase 'dependency culture' is often used to imply a criticism of a society where people expect too much. There *is* an important point here—which is that people should feel some responsibility for their own health care, income and housing. But this crucial assertion often gets lost in a general scorn of vulnerability and weakness. Both words should be used carefully and with awareness that there are different kinds of dependence and independence and that things are not always what they seem. First, even the most dependent human being can also exhibit remarkable toughness. To give only two examples, tiny infants have survived for days in earthquake and disaster conditions which have killed older children and adults. Adults whose disabilities mean they cannot walk nevertheless take part in marathon races. Second, even the weakest human beings contribute to relationships and change the people they meet. Often the tables are turned and it is no longer quite so easy to say who is dependent and who independent, who the giver and who the receiver. The child psychologist Winnicott puts it well when he says that children bring up their parents.[7] Many of those who work most closely with people who are profoundly mentally handicapped speak humbly of what they have learnt and how again and again they have been reminded of their own limits. Already there are powerful stories of how people accompanying men and women living with AIDS have themselves gained and changed.

6.18 Christians will want to say that this turning of the tables, of things not being what they seem, is central to the Gospel. As Chapter 4 shows there are many occasions in the biblical stories when someone who is physically dependent is shown to be a channel of God's grace. Both the very young and the very old and frail often seem to be specially close to God, and to act as signs of how we are called to be. The child Samuel in the Temple, the children Jesus calls to him in Luke's Gospel are all dependent on adults and yet they possess an ability to listen and to discern God's call which challenges the so-called independent.

6.19   One Gospel account which shows this particularly clearly is the story of the child Jesus being brought to the Temple by his parents (Luke 2). He is a dependent infant, and he is welcomed into the Temple by two old people, Anna and Simeon. They are reaching the end of their lives. Anna has lost her husband and her childbearing ability, and Simeon knows that death is close. But this meeting of old and young, of different generations, of individuals each with a future, a present and a past, sparks an extraordinary assertion on the part of Simeon and a recognition of Jesus' uniqueness. Simeon talks about his own future and accepts willingly his approaching death. In welcoming Jesus to the Temple he gives him a history and a tradition; the child becomes an offering to the whole community. The story is also important because it gives value to old and apparently unproductive people. The Gospel, Luke suggests, is not necessarily going to be announced first to 'successful' members of the community.

Ageing and the Experience of Black Communities in Britain

6.20   At present there are three main groups among black elderly people in this country: West Indians who came to the United Kingdom in the 1950s and have worked and grown old here; Asians who came in the 1950s and early 1960s who are now reaching old age or late middle age; and Asians who came as elderly dependent relatives or as members of refugee families. Although up to now numbers have been quite small, there is a growing group of older black people reaching the age when the question of appropriate care arises.

6.21   It is important to recognise the strengths within these groups and the networks of support which exist across generations. Many of the black-led churches show a profound capacity for community involvement rooted in prayer. The spiritual awareness and the faith of people who have been brought up in a strongly religious environment can sustain and inspire others searching for stable values. Western European secularism has much to learn from the attitude of reverence and respect for elders still to be found within some black communities.

6.22   For black people growing old in Britain today there may however be special difficulties. Their minority status of race and age combine to make them particularly open to deprivation and stress. First, stresses come from the relative poverty experienced by many elderly black people. They are likely to live in inner city areas, where the quality of housing is at its lowest, where unemployment is at its worst and where caring services are patchy and overstretched.

6.23   Second, there are stresses connected with having come to live in a new country. They may be disappointed to be living out their later years in the UK: they expected to die 'back home'. They may feel that they have not realised their dreams for themselves and for their children. They were employed doing invaluable jobs, but poorly paid, and they share with many white people the dread of ending up in residential care. As Alison Norman comments, 'Even individuals who appear to have made a successful adjustment to the new environment may have feelings of loss, despair, homesickness and anger reactivated by a new stimulus such as worrying news from home, conflict with the younger generation, or a particularly distressing experience of racial harassment.'[8]

6.24   Third, many older black people are faced with new family circumstances. The strong, all-embracing extended black family, where all ages have their dignity and identity, must increasingly be seen as a stereotype. It has allowed policy makers to conclude that black people have comprehensive family support and therefore do not need services. Patterns of caring relationships may be quite different from those in the country of origin. 'Traditional modes of caring for elderly people inevitably tend to break down under the impact of a changed environment, cramped housing in a cold climate and the radically different cultural experience of British-born children and grand-children.'[9] One research study in the Midlands reported that there was often great unhappiness between the generations: 'Whilst some middle-aged couples were as a matter of course caring for their elderly parents, they did not expect to be cared for to the same extent by their own children, and could see problems intensifying in the future. And, in spite of the stated norm that elderly people should be cared for by their own family, there were increasing numbers of elderly Asians . . . living alone.'[10] A further piece of research explored elderly Caribbean couples' views on the difference between the treatment of older people in England and the West Indies: 'A strong sense of loss pervades the replies recorded to this question—the loss of close family and community ties, and of respect for the older person. Whether the characterisation of life in the West Indies was true at the time these people left, or is true today, is less important than the *belief* that it is so. The replies also carried a strong indication that the community spirit of the West Indies could not be created in this country.'[11]

6.25 Various strategies are needed to address these problems. Statutory and voluntary agencies are beginning to recognise that black elderly people need welfare services, and are beginning to see that special provision, such as day care centres, or special diets, are sometimes necessary. The response has been most effective in areas where minority groups have been able to organise and represent their interests, where consultation has been broad and genuine and where black people have been involved in planning and implementation.

6.26 Progress is being made but it is slow. A report in 1986 from the Standing Conference of Ethnic Minority Senior Citizens (SCEMSC) concludes that 'statutory and voluntary agencies alike have failed to recognise that there are special cultural, religious and linguistic needs in so far as the ethnic minority is concerned. On a number of levels, services are planned with only the indigenous population in mind.'[12]

Risks and Rights

6.27 The very nature of human life—its preciousness and its fragility—means that throughout our lives we are confronted by risks. Parents become acutely aware of the risks such as serious illness or abuse to which their young children may be exposed. Concern extends through the pre-school years, then at school and into adolescence. At all stages there are potential risks within the home, or the school, in the street, in games and recreation, and among companions about whom the child's parents may feel some unease. All of these fears are heightened where a child or young adult is affected by any impairment of the senses or other disabling condition. The parents' concern is both for the physical protection of the child and for its mental and emotional well-being. An innate and important aspect of nurturing children is that which seeks protection from risk or the prevention of accidents. Parents anticipate their children's needs as best they can and make decisions about the acceptable levels of uncertainty or risk.

6.28 Transition to adulthood means that individuals mostly create their own risks. There is always the possibility of accidental harm which is largely ignored in day to day living. Over and above this people choose to engage in a rich variety of risky activities: sports, marriages and new jobs are but a few examples.

6.29 With increasing age the possibilities for risk taking become limited. Physical frailty may be an inhibiting factor, as may poverty, but boundaries are often set by others. People become protective of their elderly relatives or friends. They urge them to wrap up warmly in cold winds, to be careful of uneven pavements, to think twice about taking that holiday abroad, not to go out at night, not to dig the garden or paint the house. This may demonstrate care and responsibility for a person but may also undermine their autonomy.

6.30 For older people living on their own or in a household with others, safeguards against risk are necessary, but a distinction may need to be made between risk to self and risk to the safety of others. Care with clothing, with the use of water, fuel, food, medicines, mobility within the home and the local environment—all of these require vigilance. This is especially so in the case of gradual Alzheimer's Disease. Yet for many old people daily risk is confronted and most frequently overcome.

6.31 When a person moves into a hospital, nursing or residential setting, whether temporarily or permanently, great sensitivity is required from relatives, friends and caring staff. Relinquishing one's home can have profound physical and psychological effects. The surrender of many personal responsibilities, and decision-taking, including the financial ones, can be hard to accept. Sensitive decisions also have to be taken by carers about the kind of risks the person should be able to take. Some residential homes are so anxious not to expose the people in their care to risk that they do not allow them to leave the premises without supervision. This may be for the convenience of the carer. Alternatively, they may fear allegations of neglect, even perhaps prosecution, if a resident is lost, harmed or dies. On the other hand, the elderly person may perceive, however dimly, that to take risks, whatever the consequences, may be better than continuing in a protected and limited existence.

6.32   This subject has been addressed by the major national bodies in the field of old age. Some of the problems have been set out by Alison Norman, formerly of the Centre for Policy on Ageing, in her booklet *Rights and Risks*. [13] She draws attention to the pressures on some elderly people arising from over-protective anxiety on the part of relatives and others. She also deals with some of the formal constraints which have, by law, to be imposed when a person's mental health breaks down. Even more importantly, in describing the balance of ultimate risks and rights, she draws attention to the patient's consent to treatment, when gravely ill, and asks whether there should be an ultimate 'right to die'.

Conclusion

6.33   This chapter has challenged some of the prevalent attitudes to ageing. There are the negative views on the ageing process itself and the ideas that dependence is necessarily bad, that black communities have no need of special services because of their strong informal networks of care, and that elderly people should be protected from risk at all costs. These are all in their way manifestations of the same theme, namely who assumes power over whom. We shall return to this when considering the ways in which the state and the Church regard and treat older people. In contrast, the following chapter reflects on the quality and variety of opportunities which may be presented with the passage of time.

Chapter 7

ADVANCING YEARS: SOME POSSIBILITIES

7.1   As we age, so our responsibilities change. We are freed from some and assume others. The rearing of children, their departure from home, or marriage, the long-term care of a partner or relative and their eventual death are but some examples representing both loss and gain. Relinquishment of some responsibilities may be accompanied by guilt or sadness. At other times, there may be profound relief, the chance to rest or the realisation that freedom may bring new opportunities.

7.2   In this chapter we examine the opportunities for life-enhancement which can be achieved in periods of relative freedom from responsibility. First, we touch on ways in which people can expand their own horizons. Second, we reflect on the joys which new relationships can give. Then we look briefly at the part which people in later life can play in enriching the lives of the communities in which they find themselves.

Expanding the Horizons

REVIEWING LIFE

7.3   Freedom from certain types of responsibility offers space to make sense of the past and plan for the future. Talking about the events of our lives can affirm a sense of progress and wholeness. The value of reminiscence is that, even when what is being revealed relates to difficult times or unhappy experiences, it can help to maintain a sense of purpose or self-esteem and can reveal what has made that person unique. The experiences of past and present are bridged. Thinking and talking about the future is made easier. What appears to be the uncertain residue of life can be transformed into a time of personal, spiritual growth and new, or renewed, religious conviction. In the context of this review of life it is possible for there to be a daily renewal of the person through reaching out to the unseen, over and above the realities which our senses reveal. We may become attuned to things other than those which are temporal and substantial and be able to focus on the other, the holy.

'Christian faith, which relativises the past and the future, should be releasing people to speak realistically, respectfully and religiously about their own (shared) experience—of all sorts. This also brings the function of deep listening into the centrefold of theology. Why is this central category of ordinary experience—so extraordinary—so gagged and unexpressed?'[1]

7.4   For the non-believer too, reminiscence and the sharing of life's difficulties help to explain and interpret the past. This process can offer strength with which to contemplate the future. At all ages an individual needs to set a balance between activity and contemplation. Respite from material concerns, especially in the later years of life, can allow people to become relaxed and imaginative.

7.5   Unless we are to 'hesitate and falter life away',[2] there is great value in planning for the future, in deciding how the next years of life are to be spent. This may mean learning a new skill, planning for retirement, moving house or changing jobs, for example. Domestic arrangements may have to be reviewed in the light of how easy they will be to manage when energy decreases. Some basic administration may need attention—like making a will, or ensuring that a trusted friend or relative knows who to contact in time of illness or death, and the type of funeral desired.

7.6   There is growing interest in the idea of 'advance declarations' about the receipt of medical treatment at the end of life. The British Medical Association's report on Euthanasia gives the following example: 'To my family, to my physician—Should the occasion arise in my lifetime when death is imminent and a decision is to be made about the nature and extent of the care to be given to me and I am not at that time able to express my desires, let this statement serve to express my deep, sincere, and considered wish and hope that my physician will administer me simple, ordinary medical treatment. I ask that he or she will not administer heroic, extraordinary, expensive or useless medical care or treatment which in the final analysis will merely delay, not change, the ultimate outcome of my terminal condition.'[3] The inclusion of this statement should not disguise the fact that there is a great diversity of opinion about the making and use of advance declarations. What is certain is that the way we approach and plan for the end of our lives will be the subject of a major ethical debate.

STAYING WELL

7.7   Some people remain well for the major part of their lives. Others are prone to illness and premature death. The chances of staying well are closely linked with social class and with geographical variations in the distribution of disease. Nevertheless, well-being can be actively assisted in various ways. Knowledge about what may happen with increasing years and how to overcome the worst effects will do much to allay fears.

7.8   For everyone the process of ageing is likely to be accompanied by a curiosity and concern about physical bodily changes. Questions like 'Who am I?' and 'What's happening to me?' recur at every stage of life. Our responses to the signs of bodily change are part of our personal development.

7.9   In childhood there is the gradual development of physical skills, followed by an increasing awareness of personal characteristics, the signs of puberty and growth in adolescence. Later, there is the stabilising of face and physique in early adulthood and, for many, the experience of child bearing and the nurture of children. Whether physical changes are welcomed or feared depends a great deal on the attitude of peers and family and on how much openness accompanies what is happening. For example, an adolescent girl who has been prepared for her first menstrual period, and who knows in advance at least a little of what will happen to her, is more likely to feel excited about the changes taking place in her body than a girl for whom the whole subject has been shrouded in secrecy. If menstruation has been treated as an unmentionable and perhaps even dirty subject, the start of a girl's physical maturity can be a terrifying experience.

7.10   Then, in the middle years there is a realisation of many personal, physical changes, the occurrence of minor ailments, and the accumulating signs and experiences of the self that is ageing. The child-become-adult still lives, but senses may have become less acute and the body itself places limitations, not on what we are, but on how we appear and what we can achieve. Expressed in such physical terms, the latter stages of the life span may seem to present an entirely depressing prospect. 'Is all of this really happening to me?' These changes, in themselves predominantly physical, may produce profound emotional reactions in the person concerned, and can affect relationships with family, friends and colleagues.

7.11 Never before has so much information been available about the benefits of exercise and proper diet, the need to limit alcohol and smoking, and the need to avoid undue stress. The growth in over-50s keep-fit classes and special swimming sessions is a reflection of the desire on the part of many people to remain well. Important to the reduction of stress has been the growth of counselling which aims to help people deal with past or current hurts, and gain confidence about events in the future. Psychotherapy, sex therapy, and family therapy, for example, are directed towards the setting right of relationships and enhancing their quality. Bereavement counselling, redundancy counselling and retirement counselling help people to cope with loss, and to face the future positively.

7.12 The importance of preventive medicine is being increasingly recognised by health professionals. As part of their new contracts, General Practitioners are being encouraged to provide regular screening for certain conditions. Nevertheless participation in such programmes remains voluntary. Health education is a significant adjunct to the National Health Service in terms of encouraging people to make use of the services which are provided and also of making them aware of what they can do to increase their chances of staying well. The Health Education Authority, formerly the Health Education Council, has been in existence since 1987, and has produced popular material on the potential benefits of screening of various kinds, and on the prevention of illness such as heart disease.

7.13 An area of growing interest within society generally is the relationship between professionals and clients, and that between doctors and patients is no exception. Increasingly, doctors are being encouraged to explain what is wrong and offer remedies in words that can be easily understood by the person seeking help. Where options for treatment are available these should be described. The participation of the patient in the choices surrounding treatment may well lead to quicker recovery or greater understanding and acceptance of an irremediable condition.

CONTINUING LEARNING

7.14 One of the most positive aspects of living longer is the opportunity for continuing learning. Many of the submissions to the working party emphasised how much enjoyment there is in taking up new activities in later life. These opportunities are both formal and informal. At the formal level, older people can join classes run by the extramural departments of the universities and the Open University, as well as courses provided by local education authorities. Statistics about the participation of older people are not readily available but in 1981 seven per cent of the students of the Open University were over 60 years old.[4]

7.15 At an informal level, older people have organised opportunities for themselves. The University of the Third Age is probably the best example of this. The concept originated in France and there are now 160 universities in Europe, mostly for people who have retired from paid employment. Whereas in France links have been fostered with conventional universities, this pattern has not been adopted in Britain where members themselves undertake both teaching and learning. Success depends on the willingness of participants to share their skills or areas of expertise. A small fee allows local groups to advertise, to hold enrolment fairs and produce newsletters, for example.

7.16 Although many discover the enormous pleasure that is to be gained in developing new skills or building on those previously acquired, some elderly people find participation difficult. They may be reluctant to leave their homes other than in daylight hours. The timing of classes or the use of distance learning techniques, including tapes and videos, radio and television, may be helpful in these circumstances. In some areas, voluntary groups provide an escort service to classes, and seek to put people with similar interests in touch with one another. Sometimes tutors, perhaps volunteers, visit housebound people to teach them new skills. The effects of involvement can be startling. For example, some work was done in an American nursing home where 67 patients were classified as 'heavy care'. As a result of restorative activities, the number so classified a year later had been reduced to nine.[5]

7.17 There has been a great deal of debate about the decline in learning abilities among older people. It is difficult to devise tests which can provide adequate conclusions. Simple comparison between the abilities of groups of 20-year-olds and 70-year-olds ignores their very different educational and life experiences, and their motivations. Learning ability may be fundamentally affected by declining efficiency of hearing and sight, and accompanying depression in many cases. Physical fitness and health can also affect mental activity.

7.18   Adult educators have indicated that older learners do best if they can set their own pace and their own goals. Their last formal education may have consisted of rote learning, so attention will have to be given to teaching techniques which will help people and not raise barriers. Adult educators also have to be aware of their own possible prejudices; research has shown, for example, that some educators tend to avoid challenging older learners' views, and that they are likely to give attentive and polite hearing rather than to encourage the learner to engage in dialogue.[6]

New Relationships

GRANDPARENTS

7.19   A further positive aspect of older age is the opportunity it can give for delight in family relationships and friendships, and for continuing giving and receiving. Although there is little research into the role of grandparents in families, there can be a special quality to the grandparent/grandchild relationship. Many grandparents bear witness to the pleasure of a close bond without the direct responsibility of parenthood and for many children the presence of loving grandparents is enormously important.

7.20   Grandparents often offer practical support to families. For example, a survey undertaken in 1984 showed that 44 per cent of pre-school children, whose mothers were in full-time employment, were cared for by their grandmothers, usually their mothers' mothers.[7] Such care depends on proximity. In a highly mobile society, many grandparents have to find ways of developing relationships with grandchildren who are seen only infrequently. The telephone can provide a partial solution but this possibility is denied to the one-third of households of pensionable age which do not have a phone.

7.21   Changing patterns of family life, in particular the incidence of divorce and remarriage, mean that relationships between generations are increasingly complex. New partnerships and marriages restructure fundamentally the links between generations. Sometimes the pain of divorce is such that one partner feels it necessary to separate from the whole of his or her ex-partner's family, and not allow children to see grandparents. There have been some positive responses to these changes. Voluntary organisations such as the Family Rights Group and the Grandparents Federation have campaigned effectively for more attention to be given to the needs and rights of grandparents. They have argued that grandparents should be taken into account when children are taken into care or when they are going to be fostered or adopted. The organisation Stepfamily provides an advice, information and counselling service for stepfamilies and maintains over 40 self-help groups throughout the country.

SEXUALITY

7.22   One of the cruellest and most distorted expectations is that, while young people are active sexually, older people happily dispense with any expression of sexual feeling. Both young and old are diminished by this attitude and by related prejudices.

7.23   The possibility of establishing new intimate relationships should never be discounted solely on the grounds of age. Although there may be an expectation that elderly people will become non-sexual, there have been positive changes in recent years. One is the greater willingness at all ages to understand sexuality broadly, and to move away from narrow definitions focused on 'genital sexual activity', and 'sexual performance'. It is encouraging that sexuality is beginning to be seen in the wider context of our needs for intimacy and closeness.

7.24   Greater knowledge and new attitudes towards sexual expression among older people are leading to the gradual recognition of the importance and beneficial effects of continuing sexual activity for as long as possible. For many couples, enjoyment of being together is expressed as much through close bodily contact and touch as through sexual intercourse. A recent publication from Age Concern called *Living, Loving and Ageing* (1989) contains valuable material about how to overcome certain problems associated with old age, how to keep fit and how to make new relationships.

7.25   Nevertheless, people do experience difficulties as they age. Preoccupation with a career or money, redundancy, too much food or drink and monotony in sexual relations, may result in a loss of sexual interest. Some illnesses or conditions, such as Parkinson's disease or arthritis, may make intercourse difficult. For women, the menopause may bring its own particular difficulties. As people age so they may become less confident about their sexual attractiveness. The marriage partners of people suffering from dementia often find the price to pay for their loyalty extremely high. Brain impairment can cause the spouse to demand sexual activity frequently or inappropriately. The partner may find it well-nigh impossible to enjoy a sexual relationship when so many other aspects of the relationship have changed drastically.

7.26   Some people choose celibacy for all or part of their lives. A few may be scarred by childhood experiences which make them shun close relationships and others may be frightened of physical intimacy. Others may regard their celibacy as vocation, a calling to devote their energies primarily to God and others. Some simply may not have met someone with whom they wish to form a close permanent relationship.

7.27   At any one time a considerable proportion of the population is single. This reflects an increase in the age of marriage and contemporary patterns of divorce and remarriage. It is all too easy for the Church to regard the single state merely as an interval before marriage, which is held to be the ideal, rather than to be valued in its own right. Little or no attention is given to honouring the milestones in single people's lives, or in affirming their sexuality. Celebrating the single state does not mean abandoning the Church's teaching on marriage; it does mean taking seriously the confidence that God is present in people's lives in all their rich variety and in the different choices which they make.

7.28   Just as heterosexual partnerships exhibit varying degrees of commitment or permanence, so do homosexual relationships. Older homosexual people are probably less likely than younger people to acknowledge either their sexual orientation or the existence of a partner. Prior to 1967 relationships had to be kept secret because of their illegality and even now some social pressure for secrecy remains. This may put great strain on such relationships, particularly through the inability of partners to acknowledge one another publicly, or be acknowledged as a household and included in social gatherings. Some people discover their true sexual orientation only later in life and may face enormous adjustments within their existing relationships.

7.29   Relationships in old age will usually end with the death of one partner and the loss of companionship, affection and physical intimacy. Adjusting to such a loss is a long and difficult process. For some homosexual people, such adjustment is particularly hard since secrecy about the relationship may not permit open grieving.

FRIENDSHIPS

7.30   The Church has said much about marriage as a source of growth and nurture, but little about the way that friends can support and challenge each other over the years. This is especially important in later life, when many people find that their need for intimacy becomes less focused on one partner and less sexual in expression. Friends can be a crucial way of combating loneliness. They offer people the possibility of developing their own lives, and lessen their dependence on children or relatives.

7.31   Attitudes to touch have been changing for the better. More is understood about the value of physical contact in affirming people or comforting them. A hug, or a touch on the arm can express sympathy or shared joy. For some, the only regular physical contact they may have with another person is during the sharing of the Peace at communion services.

7.32   Friendships need time for their development and maintenance. They are voluntary relationships, and the chances of friendship enduring are increased with regular contact. Friends provide emotional support. In some circumstances, they may offer extensive physical care when the need presents itself. Often clergy find that their ministry to close friends or near neighbours of someone who has died is as important as their care of relatives. Consideration needs to be given to the role of friends as well as family in planning funerals. Friends may be more aware of the wishes of the person who has died than relatives who have maintained little contact.

Participating in Communities

7.33 Almost half the adult population (44 per cent) undertake some form of voluntary activity, although most of this is on a very irregular basis. Nearly one-quarter of all volunteers belong to the 25-34 age group. The percentage of volunteers over 65 is estimated at 12 per cent.[8] Sometimes people choose to continue in employment, for which they may or may not be paid beyond reimbursement of their expenses. REACH (Retired Executives Action Clearing House) is one scheme which charities can approach for help with specific tasks. The Emeritus Register is another. The Retired and Senior Volunteer Programme run by Community Service Volunteers is for retired people over the age of 50 who want to give some time to helping the community. Projects range from helping out in art galleries and museums, taking part in environmental or tourist projects, or assisting teachers in schools. The organisation Community Service Volunteers cites one woman of 82 who teaches children at school to knit.[9] Projects like Magic Me in East London link elderly people living in residential care with children from local primary schools. Hospitals, groups catering for people with special needs such as mental handicap, meals on wheels services are always seeking volunteers. For many retired people, such activity can provide not only the opportunity for social contact but also give the same sense of self-worth that employment once did.

7.34 Finally, the political power of older people is receiving greater recognition. The British electoral system does not easily allow the clustering of people round a single issue, which has happened in the United States with the Gray Panthers. Research in this country demonstrates that party allegiance remains largely unchanged with age, and that voting diminishes as people become fearful of leaving their homes or are unable to do so through disability, or lack of transport.[10] Nevertheless, older voters do lobby Members of Parliament about matters which concern them and they may become an increasingly significant force in the future. At present people over 50 form two-fifths of the electorate. By 2005, this proportion will have risen to half.[11]

Conclusion

7.35 Advancing age does not necessarily curtail the possibilities for creative engagement with life. It is however essential for older people to adopt positive attitudes for, in the words of Jeremy Laurance, 'The greatest enemy of a happier old age is pessimism. Lowered expectations are too often self-fulfilling. We see them in neglected housing, inadequate hospital services and dismal old people's homes. Old age is not all beer and skittles. But neither is it a matter of automatic ill-health and ineluctable decline.'[12]

Chapter 8

WHO CARES? WHO SHOULD CARE?

8.1   Many people in our country are caring for a dependent person, some nurturing a child into maturity, others cherishing an adult who is vulnerable because of sickness or handicap. This chapter focuses on the millions who care for dependent elderly people. It looks at the location for care, examines who does the caring and the demands made upon them, and tries to discern why they have taken on the caring task. It explores attitudes to care within the Christian tradition. Finally it considers one particular and growing challenge—that of caring for a person with dementia. What is said here about caring for older people suggests principles of care that should apply to people of all ages.

8.2   For many centuries in Britain care for elderly people has been shared between the family and wider social networks. There has been institutional provision for frail elderly people for 900 years and the hospitals and almshouses of the medieval period survive into the present century alongside nineteenth-century workhouses and twentieth-century local authority homes. Attitudes to residential care have varied. Periods in which considerable resources, commitment, time and thought have been invested in institutions have been followed by decades of neglect and then years of reform. In the late twentieth century we are aware of the shortage of state funding, lack of central planning, and poor management which can lead to neglect, and which have led to wariness of institutional care for elderly people. The picture is not uniform however: in recent years there have been some imaginative developments and reforms which have resulted in high quality, sensitive care being made available in the voluntary, private and statutory sectors.

8.3   During the last thirty years public suspicion of institutional care has found a voice in public policy. In 1958 the then Minister of Health stated: 'The underlying principle of our services for the old should be this: that the best place for old people is in their own homes.'[1] This policy has been adopted by successive governments. From the start it was accepted that the policy was not an easy managerial or financial option and that 'elderly people living at home may need special support to enable them to cope with their infirmities and to prevent their isolation from society. As their capabilities diminish they will often require such services as laundry, chiropody, meals cooked ready for eating, and home helps. (For many older people, the home help is the most significant person in their lives, even when there is good support from family or neighbours.) Loss of mobility brings the need for friendly visiting, transport to social clubs and occupation centres and arrangements for holidays. When illness is added to other infirmities they will need more home nursing, night care and help generally in the home. In terminal illness an elderly person may for a limited period need considerable help from many of the domiciliary services.'[2] It was also accepted that when people could not remain in their own home, high quality institutional care of an appropriate kind—either temporary or permanent—should be available.

8.4   Unfortunately there has rarely been enough funding to provide such comprehensive assistance, nor sufficiently good management to ensure that services are efficiently and equitably distributed. Much more attention was paid by planners during the late 1970s and 1980s to what became known as informal care. The major responsibility for looking after frail elderly people at home was seen as being with volunteers, neighbours and relatives. In theory state help would continue to be provided to assist or to provide care when family or other carers were not available, but the ideal of basic state-funded domiciliary care could not be realised. In 1980 the then Secretary of State for Social Services stated: 'When one is comparing where one can make savings one protects the health service because there is no alternative, whereas in the personal social services there is a substantial possibility, and indeed probability, of continuing growth in voluntary care, of neighbourhood care, of self-help.'[3] A year later a White Paper devoted to issues of importance to older people admitted that 'care *in* the community must increasingly mean care *by* the community.'[4]

8.5   Only recently has the extent of this caring been revealed. In 1980 the results of a survey by the Equal Opportunities Commission indicated that there might be 1.25 million people whose lives were restricted by caring for another adult who could not live safely or comfortably without them.[5] Questions added to the 1985 General Household Survey revealed that one adult in every seven is providing voluntary care and that one household in every five contains a carer. Overall there are 6 million carers in Great Britain; 3.5 million women and 2.5 million men.[6]

8.6   Some of these carers are neighbours. In many areas bonds of kinship, neighbourliness and friendship do exist which provide the infrastructure of care. Indeed there is evidence from all parts of the country that an enormous amount of informal caring takes place. Nearly all elderly people report that they have neighbours who will help in an emergency. But in many areas, both urban and rural, social cohesiveness is being undermined by a combination of geographical mobility, increasing wealth for many and poverty for a few, and a philosophy in which the dominant social ethic is individualistic, competitive and privatised. Even in those places where informal networks do exist it is doubtful if they provide much more than emergency and rudimentary assistance. Neighbours may well care *about* each other, but the basis of neighbourliness is normally reciprocity and a certain emotional detachment. The intimate tasks of caring *for* frail elderly people are usually regarded as inappropriate for neighbours. One carer reports: 'You see neighbours shy away because of the incontinence, they're frightened. No one will sit an incontinent Grandma. Never. They'll baby-sit my grandchildren. If I'm looking after my grandchildren they'll say, "Do you want to go and do so and so, I'll look after the grandchildren for an hour or two", but nobody will look after Grandma.'[7]

8.7   Most care is provided not by 'the community' in general but by the family. This is especially true when an elderly person grows more frail or is bereaved. Almost all care for those over 80 comes from the family.[8] Eighty per cent of carers are looking after relatives.[9] It seems that there are now more people caring for adult dependent relatives than for children under five.[10]

8.8   Within the family the carers may be of the same generation as the person they are looking after. Out of an estimated sixty thousand people who care for their spouse or sibling, over a third are more than 70 years old. They may receive support from unmarried children (a tenth of elderly people in need of support live with unmarried children) or married relatives of a younger generation. Of married carers the overwhelming majority are women. A variety of surveys have indicated that although there are large numbers of men who have responsibility for a frail elderly person, women are three times more likely to be caring for someone who is severely disabled than men. A quarter of women over 25 are carers.[11]

The Experience of Caring

8.9   Anna Briggs has summarised her experience of work and research among carers in Newcastle: 'The reality of community care typically results in a married woman in her mid–fifties running two households, holding down a part–time job and suffering financially and physically. Community support services are seen as inadequate, irrelevant, or just not there.'[12] She emphasises the cost of caring. Everyone who cares voluntarily does so at some cost to themselves and to others. In 1982 it was calculated that for one particular group of women time spent caring for relatives could be costed at £2,500 per person per year. The value of earnings lost (the 'opportunity cost') was then £4,500.[13] Recent Family Policy Studies Centre calculations have shown that, assuming an hourly rate of £4 (the average cost of providing home helps in 1987), the fiscal value of the work of all six million voluntary carers is £24 billion.[14] A single woman commented: 'I used to have a very good job in the City but I gave it up two years ago. I could not work the hours they wanted. . . . My pay is much worse than my previous job and there is no pension attached to it. Society is going to penalise me in the future because I am doing what society tells me I should do. I will not have an extra pension in my old age.'[15] To the loss of present and future income must be added the extra cost of heating, special foods, laundry, adaptations to the house, transport and substitute care. Unsurprisingly, carers often suffer financial difficulties and a decline in their own well-being.[16]

8.10   Alongside the financial costs come other strains. Caring is physically laborious, particularly (since most care is undertaken by one person in a family with little support from others) when an elderly person is immobile or incontinent. One carer, looking after his severely disabled wife, commented: 'When my wife was in hospital it took four nurses to turn her; now she's at home I have to do it all on my own.'[17]

8.11   For those for whom the caring task is full time there is the loss of status experienced by all those without employment. A consultant anaesthetist, looking after his wife, said, 'What hurts most of all is that you appear to become suddenly a person whose opinions count for absolutely nothing. I mean, there I was, someone who had people's lives in my hands when they were on the operating table. Then, suddenly, no one believes what you are saying. I used to tell my sons how bad their mother was getting: you know, I'd tell them about the wandering and the incontinence. I could see them exchanging glances of disbelief. I could imagine them saying to each other "The old boy is losing his marbles" and so on—me, who'd been used to respect, even deference in my previous life. And the really awful thing is that I recognise that I've done precisely the same to patients without realising what I was doing.'[18]

8.12   Above all there is the increasing isolation. Those caring for a spouse have to come to terms with the transformation of their relationship. Disease may have ended their companionship or their friendship and those around them may assume that they no longer want or need to relate sexually. For many, caring for a partner who is confined to a single bed in the living room, it seems that marriage is over. Younger carers may seem to have different problems but may find themselves feeling equally isolated within the family. Those caring for parents or in-laws have little time left over for spouse or children, and family relationships may suffer. When the elderly person needs 24-hour attention there is particular danger. Judith Oliver reports how one wife cried when she talked of her elder daughter's pregnancy: 'She was so ill and I couldn't go and look after her. And when the baby was born, I wasn't any help. I didn't see the baby until she was well enough to travel and it was three months old by then.'[19] Pat, caring for her mother and her aunt, said, 'The most soul-destroying aspect is the sheer inescapable boredom of it, not being able to communicate properly with her, or get her to do what you want logically. Few people can understand it themselves. It makes you do and say cruel things even though you love the person . . . that's when it's dangerous. I loved her, but she unwittingly drove me to the brink—and over into violence.'[20]

8.13   Parents caring for children can anticipate the most dependent stages coming to an end and usually meet other parents through clinics, nurseries and at the school gate. Most carers of elderly people know that matters are likely to become harder not easier. Once begun, the task is likely to last for years, perhaps a lifetime. Carers also have few natural opportunities to meet others in the same position. Although some find aspects of caring very rewarding, it is clear that the stress is considerable. Many know that by providing intensive support, they are probably prolonging the life of the dependent person and thus prolonging the stress they as carers experience.

8.14 Support for carers from central and local government agencies is limited. Official reports have confirmed earlier research findings of mismanagement and underfunding.[21] Disabled people and those who care for them experience this in lack of information and support as well as in inadequate and inflexible benefits and services. The intricate structures and subtleties of demarcation between the health and personal social services (health authorities providing day hospitals, health visitors and chiropodists; social services providing day centres, home helps and occupational therapists), local variation in provision (local authority gross expenditure 1984-5 on services per person over 75 ranged from £1,009 in Islington to £637 in Wandsworth, £613 in Manchester to £219 in Sefton, £481 in Cleveland to £184 in West Sussex[22]), the complexity of the benefits system and above all the lack of any one person to act as guide and advocate for each carer mean that many are never even noticed by professional carers, even general practitioners. New National Health Service and Community Care legislation should mean that some of these structural complexities are removed, but even so little formal provision has been made for carers.

8.15 The majority of elderly disabled people receive few visits from anyone in the health or social services, or from members of voluntary groups.[23] Many carers are unable to communicate their needs: those who cannot leave the person for whom they care, those without a telephone, those not skilled in dealing with bureaucracy and the professions. Those who do receive help or benefits comment on their frequent unsuitability and inflexibility. They note particularly the limited hours of day centres, the restricted contracts of many home helps and the meagre support given to those who have carers living with them. Why, when a person is assessed for help should she or he not be re-assessed periodically? Why supply meals on wheels two days a week—what is supposed to happen on other days? Why the six-month wait before the attendance allowance is received, when no one would dream of not offering child benefit for the first six months of a baby's life? As a result many carers are left feeling unsupported and taken for granted.

8.16 The reasons for taking on the caring task are complex. A carer may begin by 'keeping an eye' on someone, or may get involved at a time of crisis during illness or after an accident. The response will be influenced by particular family circumstances (geographical proximity, the quality of relationship between the possible carers and their dependant or the material circumstances of different relatives). It will be influenced above all by status (those without work or in low-paid employment being likely to have less power to resist the claims of caring) and gender (daughters taking precedence over sons, married sons passing their responsibilities to their wives).

Women, Men and Care

8.17 A survey of single people in London revealed significant differences between expectations of male and female carers. For the men and those around them their continued employment was a priority. One said, 'I've never taken time off work because the job has to come first. If that folds up everything folds up.' Sons were given support both by their relatives (many struggling with handicaps to continue cleaning, cooking and shopping) and by the social services departments (it seems that the relatives of male carers are significantly more likely than relatives of female carers to receive meals on wheels and, when disability becomes severe, access to residential care). Women, however, were expected to put caring first. Since that put many women into conflict with their employers, 15 per cent had moved from full- to part-time work and 37 per cent had given up work altogether. Others commented that the future of their job was always in question. Whether in paid employment or not women took on the bulk of household tasks with little social service assistance.[24] Their experience reflects attitudes which affect the lives of all men and women. Although these attitudes are changing, as for example fathers take on more of the physical tasks of childcare, the expectation is still that men will care *about* their relatives, working to make financial provision for them, while women are expected to care directly *for* their relatives.

8.18 Sadly these differences in expectations can lead to both men and women neglecting important sides of themselves. Men often deny their own capacity and vocation for intimate care, projecting the nurturing qualities of sensitivity, patience and gentleness on to women. Often women *are* sensitive, patient and gentle, perhaps because they are gifted, perhaps because they have learnt the skills necessary in order to be regarded as 'good women'. As Anne Borrowdale says:

> In theory, virtue for either sex consists of a selfless concern for others, but it is not a feature of masculinity in the same way it is for femininity. Women internalise the ethic of caring in a way men do not. Whether they are doing paid or unpaid work, in the home or outside it their role is characterised by service. They are expected to care for others, lovingly and with little or no reward. . . . The woman who says 'No' when confronted with the needs of others is not simply being a selfish person, she is not being a good *woman*. A man who is insensitive and uncaring is following the masculine stereotype: a selfish person, but a normal, and therefore a good *man*. The process of denial, projection and stereotyping leaves both women and men diminished.[25]

8.19 This gender division has a double effect for women. First, there is a loss of identity. Virginia Woolf describes the phantom 'angel of the house':

> She was intellectually sympathetic. She was immensely charming. She was utterly unselfish. She excelled in the difficult arts of family life. She sacrificed herself daily. If there was a chicken, she took the leg; if there was a draught, she sat in it. In short, she was so constituted that she never had a mind or a will of her own, but preferred to sympathise always with the mind and wishes of others.[26]

8.20 Paradoxically, women may use the very thing which has caused their loss of identity as a means of gaining one. Many women take on the task of caring with pathological intensity, resisting help or holiday (and thereby increasing the dependence of those for whom they care). For them coping with caring has become the one means left of forming identity. Second, women are deprived of choice. If 'society', health professionals, her church and her family expect her to care, she will find it difficult to resist. Certainly our humanity finds fulfilment in doing things for others. But if that offering is to be of worth it must be freely given.

Attitudes to Care

8.21 In our culture we learn that we ought to care, that we ought to care particularly for our relatives, and if we are female that caring for our relatives ought to be our priority. These norms are assumed to have been derived from Judaeo-Christian ethical principles, which do indeed have care at their heart. Both the Old Testament (in the relationship between God and Israel) and the New Testament (in the relationship between Jesus and those around him) reveal the intensity, generosity and fidelity of God's care. Human beings respond not only by loving God back but by loving others, God's care becoming the standard and source for their caring. The early Church seems to have given a high priority to remembering those who cared, using the story of Jesus' self-offering as part of their worship, retelling his story of the Samaritan's love, recording many instances of carers bringing the infirm for healing (Philippians 2:1-11; Luke 10:25-35; Acts 3:1-8; 9:33, 34), instructing its members in the importance of care (1 Corinthians 13; 1 John 3:17; Matthew 25:31f) and offering care itself (Acts 2:43-47; 4:34, 35).

8.22   There is, however, in biblical teaching, an ambivalence towards the significance of the family and the role of women in providing care. In the Old Testament the patriarchal family was the basic social unit, the repository not only of care but of identity, security and property. Jesus overturned this, rejecting his parents' authority (Luke 2:41-52, despite Exodus 20:12) and distancing himself from his family (Matthew 8:19, 20; 12:46-49; Mark 3:21). He called his followers away from their families (Mark 1:20), even when those families were in need (Luke 9:59-61) and the result would be treachery and feud (Matthew 10:21-35). He formed a new family born not of blood relationship but loyalty to the will of God (Matthew 10:37; 12:50; Luke 14:25). It was a drastic separation which Jesus commanded, but the command was taken literally by the church in Jerusalem where the community seems to have obliterated the boundaries of the biological family, its generosity going far beyond care for kin and kith.

8.23   In the world of Jesus' day, family and hierarchy were intertwined. A woman found her identity as daughter, wife or mother only within the family. Along with children and slaves she was always inferior to adult males. In the community around Jesus, the end of family loyalty brought with it the end of conventional power structures. The model for discipleship was not the master or the father but the child or the slave (Mark 10:15). The disciple was as likely to be a woman as a man and the stories of carers as often about men as about women (Mark 2:3, 4; 5:22, 23). Gradually, however, family structure and hierarchy were re-asserted. Although the writers of some epistles (1-3 John) regarded the Church as replacing the family, others (Peter; 1 and

2 Timothy; Titus) made it clear that the Church should incorporate, support and regulate the biological family. These communities exhorted women particularly to works of care (1 Timothy 5:10, 16; Titus 2:4, 5). It was notions not of egalitarianism, but of family and hierarchy, images not of the Samaritan caring for the Jew, but of women caring for Jesus, which the new religion took with it as it expanded into the Mediterranean world. These are the notions which have influenced our own behaviour and have contributed to the fact that elderly people are most often cared for at home by their nearest female relative. This is not the only Christian option, however, and an examination by the Church of the vision of care recorded in the Gospels, Acts and the early Epistles might show a better way.

8.24   There are several possibilities for Christians who want to look for that better way. First, there is the need for each church to be aware of those within its congregation or its parish who are providing care. Second, there is a need for support for carers at the beginning of the task (as they start to think through the implications of the responsibility), throughout the years of caring (as carers try to cope with physical, mental and spiritual stress) and at its conclusion (usually in bereavement). Third, there is the need for Christians to work with central and local government as policies are developed. They might like to campaign on behalf of carers. National campaigns already exist: the Carers National Association proposes a carer's pension payable to all carers of working age who are unable to work because of time spent looking after someone with disability, and a Carer's Allowance to cover the actual cost of caring. The Equal Opportunities Commission is encouraging those who are campaigning against discrimination in employment. Like working mothers, carers need opportunities for flexible working and leave. Locally there is a need for resources which allow carers the opportunity to choose how much to devote to the caring task. In each area there will be a continued need both for good, state-resourced and managed domiciliary support and also high-quality residential care.

8.25   The context of care will change over the next few years. While there will be increasing numbers of very elderly people in need of care there will be fewer people available to respond to the need. Families are smaller than they were, there are fewer unmarried daughters. A growing number of younger women are in full-time work, partly because of the changing needs of the labour market.[27] In addition the high divorce rate is loosening family ties. This may bring sons into closer relationship with their parents. We do not yet know what loyalty there may be to estranged in-laws or step-parents. It is likely that the cost of caring for someone at home will increase, particularly with the introduction of the Community Charge.

8.26   Caring for a dependent person may be immensely rewarding. If those who take on the caring task are to be saved from exhaustion, depression or bitterness and to be given the chance to find caring rewarding, their contribution must be acknowledged and supported.

Dementia

8.27   One of the most difficult challenges facing anyone is that of caring for a person with dementia. Dementia is used as a general term to describe the loss of various mental functions.[28] Its incidence is not related to intelligence, occupation or social class. It is related to age, and recent research indicates that between five and seven per cent of those aged over 65, and 20 per cent of those over 80, are moderately or severely handicapped by it.[29] As the proportion of those in the population aged over 80 increases, so will the incidence of dementia, which is already the most frequent cause of mental disorder amongst elderly people. Dementia is caused by specific diseases and is not the 'natural' result of ageing.

8.28   There are two main conditions which result in the symptoms of confusion, memory loss, disorientation and intellectual impairment. The dementia which affects 70 per cent of those suffering is a progressive, and at present incurable, condition resulting in a gradual decline in the ability to remember, to learn, to think and to reason. Loss of memory is generally accompanied by loss of orientation in time and place, loss of communication skills, loss of co-ordination and loss of continence. Eventually there may be agitated and aggressive behaviour and an observed 'change of personality'. The disease normally leads to death in seven to ten years but it can progress more quickly or slowly.

8.29   *Multi-infarct dementia* arises when a number of small areas of the brain are damaged by a series of strokes. Memory co-ordination and speech may be affected, symptoms differing depending on the location of the brain damage. Generally this disease progresses in a step-like rather than a gradual fashion. Since the structural and chemical abnormalities produced by either disease are difficult to detect without invasive brain surgery, conclusive diagnosis may be impossible and the terms Alzheimer's Disease and senile (pre-senile if under 60) dementia may be used with a certain fluidity, but since other, curable conditions (including infection and depression) may mimic the symptoms of dementia, thorough medical assessment is important.

8.30   At present a minority (20-25 per cent) of elderly patients in Britain with dementia is in institutional care,[30] a far lower proportion than any other European country.[31] In some areas this is because there is a high level of support in the community, both formal and informal. In others it is partly because of a low level of provision of residential accommodation and partly because of the stigma which still adheres to residential care for confused elderly people. People relate uneasily to institutions which were once workhouses and are still mental hospitals. They know that wards are often full of very confused patients, and that some patients have been poorly, even cruelly treated. Because of the location and design of most hospitals, patients are removed from a familiar, domestic environment and thus lose the external clues which might preserve or support their identity. Unless staff are well-trained and supported, patients tend to become very confused, and staff tend to define care as care only for the body, reducing their investment in relationship with the patient.[32] Psychogeriatric units can provide valuable assessment, respite and long-term care, particularly in health districts (in 1986, two-thirds of the total), where a consultant psychiatrist has designated responsibility for elderly people. Demand is such that in some areas there are insufficient beds and people with dementia often have to be admitted to geriatric and general wards where there is little chance of expert assessment or care and where confused people are resented for 'blocking' an acute bed. Alternatively patients go to local authority, voluntary or private homes where staffing on occasions may be inadequate to cope with the special needs of people with dementia, and where other residents find their presence disturbing. According to one recent survey approximately 50 per cent of residents of old people's homes and 65 per cent of residents in geriatric hospital wards are 'confused'.[33] So great is the need that those with dementia now occupy the majority of institutional beds in Britain.

8.31   For most people, residential care remains a last resort and the majority of those with dementia live 'in the community'. In the average health district of 250,000 people, 1,800-2,500 will be moderately or severely affected by dementia. Of these 1,500-2,100 will be living at home. An average general medical practice will have 25 patients suffering from dementia, half of them severely affected and about 20 of them living at home.[34] Of those living at home approximately one-third will be living alone, slightly under a third will be living with and looked after by an elderly spouse and slightly more than a third will be living with other relatives. It is important to note that there is considerable variation in the severity of dementia—and many people in the milder stage of the disease can function with relatively little support.[35]

8.32   Dementia is frightening both for the sufferer and for those who care for them. People in the early stages of dementia will perhaps become aware that tasks like cooking or writing or knitting have become increasingly difficult and that later on they cannot remember words and then cannot put sentences together. At this stage those experiencing the disease may deny that anything is wrong, compensating by making lists and writing reminders and avoiding activities where mistakes might be made. This inevitably increases the sense of isolation and though they will manage for much of the time the exhaustion resulting from the effort of compensating for incapacity will leave sufferers depressed or angry. By this time those close to the sufferer will have begun to notice either the loss of skills or knowledge, or the occurrence of odd or disturbed behaviour and will themselves be experiencing considerable stress. Yet there may be a gap of as much as two or three years between a relative suspecting that there is a problem and contacting the doctor.[36] This can be a time of considerable uncertainty, fear and isolation.

8.33   It is not known how much a person with dementia continues to suffer emotionally as the disease progresses. It seems that distress for the person with dementia is greatest in the early stages of the illness. But for the carer distress does not wane. Following the initial uncertainty about the nature of the disease come other strains as cognitive, emotional and behavioural changes progress. Surveys have shown that the cause of greatest strain to carers is the need to acknowledge and renegotiate a change in relationship, perhaps a reversal of marital roles or, more traumatically, the inversion of the relationship between parent and child. That someone who is loved is no longer able to talk sensibly or to show any interest in their surroundings, that they are incontinent or exhibit dangerous or inappropriate behaviour, forces the care-giver to admit the change in the sufferer's identity and thus the change in relationship.[37] This change affects the whole family: half of all carers experience marriage strain and a similar proportion find they have problems with their children.

8.34 There is now some professional recognition of the strain resulting from such caring. The Royal College of Physicians reports that 'it is the strain of caring day after day with wandering behaviour, incontinence, or the inability to conduct a conversation that in the end wears down the most resilient helper.'[38] Carers themselves report feelings of grief, anger, guilt and shame.[39] The Royal College of Physicians recognises that the strains caused by dementia which are at present borne by a few must become the responsibility of us all: 'The high prevalence of organic mental impairment in the elderly and the need for the majority to be cared for in the community present one of the most pervasive social health problems of our generation. There has been little systematic effort to prepare the public or the health professions for their role in meeting the needs of the mentally impaired elderly.'[40]

8.35 Support for those with dementia living in the community is provided at present by both health (e.g., district nurses and health visitors) and personal social services (e.g., home helps and meals on wheels). Although there is a potentially large range of agencies offering practical support, the actual needs of those caring for people who are mentally infirm are not always met. The greatest needs are for relief from constant supervision and help with coping with incontinence. Home helps, day centres, day hospitals, night nurses and laundry services are overstretched and often can only offer limited support.

8.36 Many of those who tend people with dementia find that in order to survive they must distance themselves from the most acute distress. This distancing may be both emotional, caring being reduced to the purely physical since the 'real' person is felt to have died some time before, and geographical, the sufferer being taken into residential care. It has been observed that nursing staff may place those most severely affected furthest from their office and the entrance to the ward, and that visiting clergy may spend most of their time with patients most capable of dialogue. Distancing leads easily to denial. Clergy omit to mention dementia in funeral services, hospital doctors refuse to admit that there is a need for increased provision,[41] services for people with dementia are underfunded compared with acute services. Sufferers are made to disappear into 'the community' or isolated mental hospitals and frequently we think 'it would be better if s/he died'. While we may have begun to confront our fears about cancer or AIDS, dementia leaves us overwhelmed. 'By the time I arrived as a deacon he was senile and used to embarrass my inexperience and leave me not knowing what to do. I used to take him Holy Communion. At the short service I would say, "Make your humble confession to Almighty God", and instead of reciting the confession he would say, "You were at Trinity College, Cambridge, weren't you?" It was difficult to know how to proceed.'[42]

8.37   Una Kroll, writer, deaconess and retired doctor, comments:

> I have a vivid memory of the fear and disgust that overwhelmed me when, as a medical student, I visited a psycho-geriatric ward full of senile old ladies. I was inexperienced and gauche. I did not begin to know how to talk to anyone. The patient who had been assigned to my care for the day called for her mother in a high-pitched whining voice at ten second intervals for the whole morning. It was a tremendous relief when she eventually stopped whining while she gobbled up her lunch and then slumped into her chair for her afternoon sleep. When she woke up she was wet, smelly and irritable. The whining started up again, interspersed this time with a rich variety of swear words that embarrassed me. As we made our way to the bathroom door to change her clothes, one of the older nurses said to her: 'You are a naughty girl today, Rosa, playing up the young doctor like that.' Rosa stopped, swung herself round to face me, bared her gums in a ferocious grin and said in a clear voice: 'She doesn't like me and I don't like her, so there.' It was true. At that moment I wanted to run away.[43]

8.38   Our society does a lot of running away from dementia and as a result those who become carers are unprepared for their task.

> You're just assumed to be a 'natural carer'; somehow you will magically find all the necessary physical and emotional resources to cope. It's funny when you consider the effort they go to to give new mothers advice on how to handle babies—no one tells you how to handle incontinent, senile

parents that spread faeces over the walls and wander off at night. Because it's not talked about, you think you should 'know' and then in addition to all the other pressures, you feel guilty because you can't cope with it. [44]

8.39   The encounter with someone who has dementia is profoundly disturbing. It is a reminder both of human helplessness (this person reveals the limits of medical or counselling skills, and my own tolerance) and human fragility (this person reveals how easily memory and then self-awareness can disintegrate), and it raises acute questions about personhood. If 'living with dementia is coming to terms with the irreversible loss of a human being' when was that person lost? [45] A recent study on Alzheimer's Disease uses the revealing subtitle 'The Long Bereavement'. [46]

8.40   Joseph Fletcher, a writer on Christian ethics, in his recent work on personhood identifies fifteen indicators of humanness. [47] These include minimum intelligence, self-awareness, self-control, a sense of time, of future and of the past, the capability of relating to others and being concerned for them, communication, control of existence, curiosity, change and changeability, balance of rationality and feeling, idiosyncrasy and neo-cortical function. For Fletcher the ability to think and the capacity to relate are the most significant aspects of being human and he stands within a long tradition of Christian thinking which links rationality and self-awareness to being in the image of God. Thus in the liturgy and discipline of the Christian Church there has been an assumption that, in order to be full members of the community, individuals should be aware of themselves, the world and God and that they should be able to confess the faith, confess their sins and tell the story of salvation. [48]

8.41   Christian theology and the practice of the Church (with the exception of chaplaincy in psychiatric hospitals) both seem tacitly to exclude the person with dementia. Their chaos, in the sense of physical deterioration and loosened social relationships, is exacerbated by separation from the worship of the churches and perhaps therefore from a sense of the love of God. Hugo Petzsch writes:

> While it is recognised that many churches would find it practically impossible to accommodate people with dementia in their services, it is worth pondering the reasons. A sobering contrast can be drawn between the church's response to the demented and their response to young children. While both groups have in common the tendency at worst to be

91

incontinent, smelly, noisy and difficult to control, a considerable amount of energy is expended on providing special services for the young and on integrating those to some degree into the congregation's main diet of worship on Sundays. It is not difficult to imagine the initial response of most congregations to a dementing adult or elderly person who was brought to a normal Sunday service. The implications of this parallel might lead one to think that the churches are implicitly endorsing a very materialistic view of humanity. That is, that people are only of worth when they hold the ability or potential to contribute actively to society. While this is the case with children, who are seen as the hope for the future, it is patently not the case with the severely demented who, whatever they may have contributed during their life before illness, are now regarded as being incapable of contributing to society.[49]

8.42   Chapter 4 has already explored some of the biblical insights about suffering and apparent deterioration. If the Church asserts with St Paul that 'nothing in all creation will be able to separate us from the love of God in Jesus Christ our Lord' and wants those enveloped in the chaos of dementia to sense that victory, it must ensure that they are included. As its basis, the task must involve beginning to deal with the profound human fear of dementia, and must produce theoretical, symbolic and practical responses. At the theoretical level there is a need to develop an understanding of humanness which values affectivity alongside rationality. Robert Wennberg, writing on medical ethics, suggests that 'a person is in a strict sense a being who possesses the developed capacity to engage in acts of intellect (to think, use language) acts of emotion (to love, hate) and acts of will (to make moral choices, to affirm spiritual ideals).'[50] According to this definition a person with dementia is still only a person in a restricted sense, but by emphasising the emotional as a sign of personhood, Wennberg at least gives someone with dementia a partial identity. A carer has written of her own recognition of that humanity:

> Now there is no more doing—hand and eye
> Have lost their urgent creativity.
> Now there is no more seeking of applause
> For work or art or cause;
> Simply the eyes seek affirmation of her being,
> Waiting to answer smiling with a smile;
> and holding eye and smile you sense the freeing
> Love and acceptance for her deepest soul.
> 'To see her' people say 'must be distressing'
> And miss the blessing.[51]

8.43   Symbolic interpretations may also help to change attitudes. Hugo Petzsch suggests that the biblical models of the scapegoat (Leviticus 16) and the suffering servant (Isaiah 52:13-53:12) can be seen as metaphors for our relationship with those with dementia. Writing about the scapegoat, he notes its role in Israelite society in distancing the people from their sin. In our culture those with dementia are made to carry full responsibility for the breakdown in the relationship between themselves and the rest of society and are then banished from us. For Petzsch, the scapegoat is a worst-case model. The suffering servant shows awareness of suffering, indeed accepts responsibility for that suffering, while distance is maintained. This he suggests is frequently the mode of response of health professionals and report writers, in their 'informed inertia'.

8.44   Alongside these two figures Hugo Petzsch places the person of Jesus and the incident of the healing of the Gadarene demoniac (Mark 5:1-20) and a man suffering a mental illness which resulted in his being ostracised. He comments: 'Yet when he rushed towards Jesus he was not rejected, told to go away so as not to contaminate people, nor was he ignored discreetly . . . Jesus accepted him completely and unconditionally, asking his name, healing him and re-integrating him into society.' Petzsch concludes that 'as long as society persists in the distancing and informed inertia outlined in the scapegoat and suffering servant models there is little chance of a corporate acceptance of the plight of demented people which is a prerequisite of the "will to heal". Healing for people who are becoming demented means primarily unconditional acceptance which in turn will bring concern for their plight and the means or will to alleviate it.' [52]

8.45   Finally the Church should offer a practical response. Already new forms of care are being pioneered: Williamwood House, a Church of Scotland Eventide Home for confused elderly people, has developed ways of working with residents and day-visitors which ensure their dignity is upheld. [53] Action is needed at the level of local church life to enable those with dementia to be included. This will involve learning to communicate, both in pastoral contact and in worship, in a different way, emphasising the sensual and the present. All those with dementia retain some sensory function. Sight, sound, smell, touch and taste evoke strong responses. It may be thus possible for people with dementia to respond to worship and to respond to the worship of others. Candles, incense, the kiss of peace, the feel of the cross, the taste of bread and wine, familiar word-patterns in prayer and music, especially hymns, become more significant than the words of liturgy or sermon. It may be impossible for those with dementia to attend Sunday services regularly. The sufferer may be too badly handicapped or it may place an additional burden on the carer, but if prejudice is to be overcome and people with dementia are to be given adequate spiritual sustenance, they must be found a place within the body of Christ. Then when individual memory is lost, the body of Christ can remember together for them; when individual rational control is lost, the body of Christ can declare the faith together for them; and when individual identity is collapsing, the body of Christ can uphold that person and those who love them in the hope of the resurrection.

Part IV

ISSUES FOR THE NATION AND FOR THE CHURCH

Chapter 9

PUBLIC, PRIVATE AND PERSONAL

9.1   The last chapter explored the complex nature of care offered by one family member to another, and the way in which this usually defies simple categories. The relationship between carer and cared-for is rarely one-way, and even the frailest person usually gives as well as receives. The chapter also asked questions about the proper responsibilities of the family, the neighbourhood and organised professional support. It suggested that in the future family members are likely to be asked to take on more difficult long-term tasks and will therefore need much greater financial and emotional support.

9.2   This chapter moves on to care on a larger scale and considers those collective welfare services which our society has developed. Such consideration is necessary because the individual ageing process, though of course personal and unique, takes place in a social and political context. Whether or not someone can seize the opportunities of old age described in Chapter 7, depends partly on external support, on adequacy of income and on the environment in which he or she lives. We therefore look briefly at the way welfare services have developed in this country, and at the different strands of provision. We then consider what is available for elderly people and suggest some principles for future planning.

Changes in Welfare

9.3   During the first half of this century legislation was gradually enacted which brought into being what is now called the welfare state. The term has been taken to mean the collection of services, funded mainly out of taxation and run by central and local government, covering education, health, income support, personal social services and housing. The welfare state was not a new creation, but was built on a foundation of earlier social provision, which had been developed in order to deal with some of the vast excesses of deprivation. The Poor Laws, the Public Health Act 1848, Lloyd George's pension scheme of 1911, the Housing of the Working Classes Acts 1890, 1894 and 1900 provide but a few examples of increasing state intervention and regulation. Probably the greatest change brought about by legislation in the 1940s was the large-scale provision of services out of general taxation.

9.4 Since the Second World War, most people have come to accept that education for their children will be provided through state maintained schools, health care can be obtained largely free of charge at the point of delivery, benefits will be available to enable the weathering of times of hardship, and that, in a more limited way, housing can be provided by local authorities.

9.5 There have been two major challenges in the last fifteen years to the continuation of services financed through taxation. The first has to do with the cost of supporting them. It has been argued that the higher taxes required to sustain welfare provision have reduced incentives and fuelled inflation. Demand for services is unbounded, and people's expectations for care of various kinds has required a level of funding which successive governments have found hard to provide. Administrative change and financial constraints affecting staff at all levels within health and community services have served to bring to public attention the existence of limited resources, the necessity for rationing of care and the need to identify priorities.

9.6 Coupled with the resource question has been a change in the climate of opinion concerning the desirability of state involvement. It has been argued that the state has taken over many of the functions and responsibilities which the individual and family should properly cover, and that independence, choice and the need for neighbourliness have been neglected. Detailed criticisms of the concept of the welfare state were set out in the Board for Social Responsibility's report *Not Just for the Poor* (CHP 1986) and it is not intended to repeat them here. It is important, though, to assess the impact of these criticisms in relation to the emerging patterns of service provision.

9.7 Some developments are clearly positive. For example, it is good that consumer views are being taken more seriously. It is recognised that the most effective services are often those where the user is encouraged to express a view, to participate, and to be as much an equal partner as possible. Self-help groups have thrived. Professionals are now more likely to share information with their clients or patients.

9.8   Throughout the 1980s, churches have also stressed that welfare provision in this country is an achievement not lightly to be discarded and have affirmed the commitment of many of those working within the public sector. They have felt compelled to question the rationale of many of the reforms to the welfare state and to express concern about their effects. Examples of such interest are provided by the Board's evidence and response to the review of the social security system in 1985, by the Board of Education's criticisms of some of the proposals contained in the Education Reform Act 1989, and by representations made to Government by Christian voluntary organisations about the plight of homeless people.

9.9   Government policies have increasingly given encouragement to individuals to take more responsibility for their personal well-being. Tax relief on mortgage interest up to £30,000, for example, has helped many people to meet their housing needs through owner occupation. A measure of tax relief on insurance premiums and pension contributions has indicated the value placed on people providing for their own support during times of unemployment, illness or retirement. More recently, the Finance Act 1989 gave people in retirement tax relief on private medical insurance premiums, whether paid by them or by their families on their behalf. As the percentage of people in the population who are owner-occupiers rises, so arguments have been put forward that in future they should support themselves in their old age by realising the equity of their properties. There is already a range of schemes in existence whereby people may sell their properties to companies in return for continued occupation and small incomes, or can raise loans which are repaid on death and the subsequent disposal of accommodation.

9.10   It was intended by William Beveridge, who shaped new welfare legislation in the 1940s, that people in work would contribute to a state-supervised pension fund which would subsequently support them through times of hardship and in retirement. Transitional arrangements would have to be made for existing pensioners while the fund was built up. The Labour Government of 1945 decided, however, to pay full pensions immediately. This made present pensions dependent on contributions from people currently in work, thereby undermining the link between current payments and future benefits. This arrangement now has to be set against the background of a decreasing ratio of wage earners to pensioners.

9.11 The future difficulties of maintaining state benefits for older people at a reasonable level may lead to inter-generational conflict. Pensions could form the focus for immediate disagreement but an added dimension may be that people retiring in the next 20 years and expecting support will themselves have received extensive benefits from the welfare state which are now not available to those people who will be required to contribute. Loans for higher education, for example, are in part to replace grants. The value of mortgage tax relief to the prospective home buyer, while still significant, has diminished in relation to house prices. Restrictions on social security payments have made it less easy for people to claim than in the past, and generally services are less readily available. Such differences in treatment between groups in the population are likely to diminish, rather than enhance, social cohesion.

9.12 In response to the increasing emphasis being placed on individuals and families taking more responsibility for their own welfare arrangements, a range of services has become available outside those provided by the state. It is now necessary to look at the changing roles of the private and voluntary sector.

Growth in the Private Sector of Welfare Provision

9.13 Private services have burgeoned in recent years mainly in London and the South-East. The number of beds in independent hospitals and nursing homes, for example, has doubled since 1971, while the number of people subscribing to private health insurance has almost trebled to 5.3 million over the same period.[1] One of the most striking areas of growth is the establishment of independently run residential homes for elderly people. Between 1980 and 1985, the number of places in private residential establishments doubled to 70,000.[2]

9.14 It is argued that because people are paying for a service, they have greater choice and control about its quality and the manner in which it is provided, and the freedom to seek alternative suppliers. In practice, however, there are several questions which have to be asked about the reality of private provision when compared to the theoretical benefits. For example, despite examples of excellent practice, the presence of unskilled and untrained staff is greater in private homes than in those in the public sector, and can lead to low standards of care. Consumers of services may be frail, unwilling to demand better attention or different treatment through fear of ill-treatment or neglect.

9.15   Some service provision regarded as part of the private sector is essentially non-profit making. Other enterprises are run for profit, which may make for efficiency but can also lead to reduction in the quality of service. It is worth noting that the business failure rate of private care establishments and the high rate of staff turnover introduces a hazardous element for people when they are at their most vulnerable. The independent sector cannot escape the regulatory function of the state, whereby standards are set for the services provided. Residential homes for elderly people are regulated through qualification requirements and inspection, although those establishments with four or less residents have thus far been exempt. Private pension schemes and sick pay arrangements must conform to standards laid down by the state, and so can be fundamentally affected by changes in legislation.

9.16   It is difficult to envisage that private provision could ever replace public provision in its entirety. There are some activities undertaken by the public sector which are not attractive financially and thus will be avoided by the independent sector. Private health insurance schemes may restrict the range, duration, or cost of care covered in order to avoid the unlimited expenditure required by long-term care. Nevertheless, it is likely that the private sector will continue to receive attention as a means of diminishing the cost of welfare services provided by the state.

The Contribution of the Voluntary Sector

9.17   The voluntary sector defies easy definition since a wide variety of activities falls within its compass. It includes both large bodies with highly qualified, paid staff and small groups of people who come together to achieve one objective, perhaps within a short period of time. They range from complex organisations like housing associations to local church lunch clubs and play groups.

9.18   Voluntary organisations can to some extent complement statutory provision by offering services which might not otherwise exist. They are often freer than statutory services to deal with issues in new ways. Conversely, some voluntary agencies have been rigid in their styles of operation and have been slow to recognise that the services offered were no longer relevant to social needs. Although co-ordination with other organisations does exist in many places, this is not necessarily so, and duplication of effort does sometimes occur. Tensions can also be experienced between professional paid staff and volunteer helpers. Nevertheless, the voluntary sector does provide an important alternative to both public and private sector provision.

9.19   Recent Government policies have envisaged that in future voluntary agencies will play a much greater role in the mixed economy of welfare and in scrutinising both the cost and quality of services. The Housing Act 1988, for example, has given opportunities for housing associations to assume control of local authority estates, subject to the consent of the tenants. The proposals for relating to the expansion of care for people in the community assume that voluntary agencies will make an important contribution.

9.20   There are two areas of concern which may make it difficult for the voluntary sector to fulfil these expectations even when they believe that it is appropriate for them to do so. First, there is the question of funding. Part of the income for most voluntary organisations consists of grants from central and local government, but these have become less readily available in recent years. Voluntary organisations have therefore been encouraged to engage in additional fund raising and this tends to divert energy from their original purpose. Grant-making bodies report major increases in the numbers of requests for help. Some types of agency have been enabled through legislation to borrow money on the open market. Servicing such loans and making repayments requires the imposition of higher charges for the services provided, which may place them outside the reach of the very people for whom the voluntary organisation was created.

9.21   Second, for those organisations which rely on volunteer rather than paid staff there may be problems in future in recruitment. The Volunteer Centre has recently drawn attention to the likely decrease in the number of volunteers, as the participation of women in the labour force increases to make good the shortage of young people by providing basic goods and services.[3] For both these reasons it would be unwise to rely on the voluntary sector to play a major role in providing services.

9.22   The role of the Church as a voluntary organisation is considered in Chapter 10. What is clear is that caution is needed before embarking on new projects. Much voluntary activity is subject to the same regulations and inspection as is applied to the private sector. Churches which wish to set up schemes may find that their buildings are unsuitable for the use they have in mind or require costly re-ordering. Organisers may require thorough training provided by professionals, and services must meet the required standards. There are many excellent examples of church-based schemes but they require costly commitment in order to be successful.

The Range of Services for Older People

9.23 The following sections outline and assess the kinds of provision which already exist for older people in the statutory, private and voluntary sectors in the areas of income maintenance, housing, personal social services, health and education.

Income Maintenance

9.24 It was noted earlier that older people as a group are perceived as exercising considerable consumer power through rising incomes. The average income of people of pensionable age rose by 31 per cent in real terms over the period 1979-1987.[4] Individual incomes are most likely to be made up from a combination of retirement pensions, occupational pensions, income from savings, earnings and social security benefits. The table below shows the relative importance of each of these categories to an average income in 1987.

Table 3

Pensioners' Incomes *			
	1979	1987	Real terms increase 1979-1987
Total Social Security Benefits	50.50	50.20	17%
Occupational Pensions	13.20	23.30	77%
Savings Incomes	9.10	20.90	130%
Earnings	9.90	7.90	−20%
Total Gross Income	82.80	111.20	34%
Total Net Income	75.90	99.90	31%

*£s per week at 1987 prices. Source: *Family Expenditure Survey*.

9.25   The basic national insurance pension for April 1989 to April 1990 was £43.60 for a single pensioner and £69.80 for a couple. Up to the end of the 1950s, National Insurance pensions were raised roughly in line with prices. During the 1960s, rises in wages were also taken into account so that contributory and non-contributory benefits would reflect the general increase in prosperity. Subsequent linkage in 1980 to price increases only has led to a widening gap between pensions and earnings which have risen faster than the rate of inflation. Median weekly earnings for all males stood at £215 in 1988.[5] There is evidence to suggest that other European countries spend much higher proportions of their national incomes on retired people than is the case in Britain.[6]

9.26   Statistics about average incomes can be used to obscure the realities of income distribution between groups of pensioners. It is true, for example, that over 80 per cent of pensioners are in receipt of occupational pensions but whereas for the top 20 per cent of households ranked by income, occupational pensions contributed an average of £8,600 in 1986, they contributed nothing to the incomes of the lowest 20 per cent and only £150 per annum to the next lowest 20 per cent.[7] Social security benefits, on the other hand, contributed £930 per annum to the lowest 20 per cent declining to £200 for the top 20 per cent.[8] The figures in 1986 for total gross income showed that 60 per cent of households in the lowest income groups had annual incomes of less than £4,000 while those in the top 20 per cent had over £11,500.[9] There are vast differences in the levels of income received by pensioners, added to which there is a differential rate of growth. Over the period 1979 to 1986 incomes in the poorest fifth rose by 20 per cent whereas incomes in the top 20 per cent rose by 27 per cent.[10]

9.27   In 1987, 73 per cent of pensioners received income from savings.[11] Savings represent security for many older people. They ensure a way of meeting unexpected bills, or maintaining property, or financing residential care and ultimately funerals. Recent changes to the benefits systems have meant that older people with substantial savings but low incomes, who received benefits under the old schemes, have found themselves worse off under the new regulations. The modification of Housing Benefit and the implementation of the Income Support scheme provide two examples.

9.28   An earlier paragraph indicated the importance of social security benefits to the income of less well-off groups of pensioners. Housing

Benefit is available for help with rents. The level of benefit is assessed on the ability of people to meet their rent payments, which depends on the levels of their incomes and savings. Changes to the regulations relating to income and savings levels were changed in 1988 and resulted in over three million pensioners losing some benefit, including 750,000 who lost all entitlement, while 990,000 gained.[12] The effects of the introduction of the Community Charge are not yet clear.

9.29　In 1985, the Government announced its plans for reforming the social security system.[13] The intentions—to reduce the complexities of the existing structure, to target resources more effectively and to increase self-reliance—were welcomed by many people. Under the old Supplementary Benefit system, people received a basic benefit which could be enhanced by claiming additional weekly allowances to meet special needs for diet, heating or laundry for example. Help was also available for water rates, insurance and house maintenance costs. The new Income Support system simplified this by giving personal allowances with flat rate premiums for certain groups of people, including pensioners or people with disabilities. Help with water rates has been withdrawn, and people must pay 20 per cent of their rates or community charge. In 1988-9, 27 per cent of all single people and 9 per cent of couples of pensionable age were in receipt of income support.[14]

9.30　Perhaps the biggest difference for older people has been the introduction of the Social Fund to meet needs which formerly had been covered by the special allowances. Payments from the Fund are discretionary whereas the old system gave legal entitlement. In addition, payments from the Fund are most usually given as loans which must be repaid within eighteen months, or two years in exceptional circumstances. Grants are available to promote community care and can be paid to help people after a stay in residential or institutional care, or to help people to remain in their own homes. Age Concern undertook a survey in 1989 which showed that, among the older people who attend Age Concern groups, most would rather suffer hardship than ask for loans.[15] There has been an increase in requests to charities for help. Generally there is a lack of awareness about the community care grants provision of the Social Fund.

Housing

9.31 The majority of people of pensionable age live in private households. The 1981 Census showed that only 5 per cent resided in sheltered accommodation, and only 300,000 were in any form of institutional care. Many older people live alone, particularly the most elderly. In 1985, 58 per cent of women over 75 lived by themselves compared with 26 per cent of the men in the same age range.[16]

9.32 The 1985 General Household Survey showed that 61 per cent of all households with one or more adults over 60 were owner-occupiers, 30 per cent rented from a local authority or housing association, and that 7 per cent were in the private rented sector. The English House Condition Survey 1986 showed that over three-fifths of properties lacking basic amenities and nearly two-fifths of unfit properties were occupied by people aged 60 or above. Often older people are deterred from having their properties repaired by the cost, the prospect of upheaval during building work and the fear of bad workmanship. In order to combat some of these difficulties agency services have been set up in some areas. These offer advice to elderly people about the nature and extent of the work required, help them to obtain adequate building services and also to organise funding and support while the work is being done. Many agency services are run by voluntary bodies with some funding from the Department of the Environment.

9.33 It is an aim of Government policy to enable people to stay in their own homes for as long as possible. The details of the Community Care programme are covered later in this chapter. Important to elderly people is the ability to summon help. There are several kinds of alarm schemes ranging from cards which can be placed in windows to highly sophisticated signalling devices linked to a central point with constant cover. These often form part of wider care arrangements, which may include neighbours or street wardens who are committed to visiting older people on a regular basis, and perhaps undertaking simple tasks. In return, helpers receive a small wage or honorarium.[17]

9.34 As people become more frail, they may seek accommodation which is easily managed or where extra support is readily available. The term 'sheltered' housing covers a range of schemes, which vary according to their size, range and quality of services and facilities, and the amount of community activity. Resident wardens are available in many schemes to summon help in times of emergency. In others meals may be provided and help given with domestic tasks. The need for 'very sheltered' accommodation (that is sheltered housing with extra care facilities such as meals) as a means of allowing people to maintain independence is receiving increasing recognition.[18] There are a small but growing number of schemes where nursing or medical help is available, sometimes from an adjacent nursing or residential home. Sheltered housing schemes have been provided by local authorities, private developers and housing associations. Units may be purchased outright on a shared equity basis, or rented.

9.35   The 1948 National Assistance Act puts local authorities under a statutory obligation to provide residential accommodation for 'persons who by reason of age, infirmity or any other circumstances are in need of care and attention which is not otherwise available to them'. Numbers of places in local authority homes have not increased since 1979, despite demographic pressure.[19] Over the same period the number of places in private and voluntary homes (seemingly more attractive since they are often smaller, less isolated and better appointed than state institutions) has doubled.

9.36   Residents whose resources fall below the limits set for the receipt of Income Support payments are entitled to help with fees from the social security system. Various surveys have shown that the charges for residential and nursing homes are often higher than the limits on social security payments.[20] There has been growing concern in recent years about the likelihood of eviction where neither residents nor their families can make good the deficits between fees charged and payments received.

Personal Social Services

9.37   Local authorities are expected to provide a wide range of welfare services for people in need at all ages. For elderly people these include home help services, meals on wheels, occupational therapy, holidays and outings, day centres, and transport schemes, as well as residential care schemes described above.

9.38   Over the next few years the way that welfare services are delivered to frail and needy people living in the community are to be reorganised. The roles of the voluntary and statutory and private sectors will change. The National Health Service and Community Care Act 1990 seeks to give local authorities clear responsibilities to make sure that individuals with particular needs for care—because of mental illness, mental handicap or disability—receive the services they need. Rather than necessarily providing the services directly, local authorities may acquire them from private or voluntary agencies. How the new system develops will have a substantial effect on the lives of older people.

9.39   It is not our place here to comment in detail on this reorganisation. However, some features are clearly crucial. First, local authorities must be given adequate resources to carry out their new tasks. Second, the very welcome emphasis that the White Paper on Community Care made on the support needed by carers must be sustained. Third, the stress on flexibility and on choice must be accompanied by a commitment to monitor standards across the country.

9.40   A key concept is the understanding of *need*—need for care, need for services and who makes the assessment of need. Does the individual assess his or her own need, or does someone else make the assessment—such as a professional or a person (perhaps a family member) who has a responsibility for caring (either chosen or imposed by necessity)? How possible will it be for assessments to be challenged?

9.41   Another key issue is the balance between the services that are offered directly or indirectly by personal social service departments, in the home, in day centres and in residential establishments. Recent years have seen a greater readiness to move away from considering residential services in isolation, and to see them rather as part of the continuum of care in the community. There has also been more recognition of the fears surrounding institutional life, partly because of its association with the workhouse. 'The prospect of entry to a residential establishment touches a deep-seated fear of being inescapably cast alone and defenceless among strangers, especially strangers whose codes are unknown but assumed to be disturbingly different from one's own.'[21] On the other hand, for many the residential establishment can become a warm and supportive community.

9.42   Many residential establishments have suffered from tight budgets and less than adequate physical conditions. Staff morale has also often been alarmingly low. Crucial though environment, diet, leisure activities in the home are, the ability of staff to respond sensitively to residents' needs seems to be one of the most important factors in residents' sense of well-being.

9.43 In 1985 an independent review of residential care was commissioned by government, to 'review the role of residential care and the range of services given in statutory, voluntary and private residential establishments within the personal social services in England and Wales; to consider, having regard to the practical constraints and other relevant developments, what changes, if any, are required to enable the residential care sector to respond effectively to changing social needs, and to make recommendations accordingly.'[22] When the committee, chaired by Lady Wagner, reported, it used the memorable title *A Positive Choice* to describe the best approach to residential care. The report declared: 'People who move into a residential establishment should do so by positive choice, and living there should be a positive experience.' It looked at the needs of staff and commented that 'the complex and often stressful nature of the work needs to be recognised as staff must have proper support and training'. It also evolved a series of principles (reproduced in Appendix A) which emphasise choice, residents' rights and participation. Great vigilance is going to be needed in the years ahead to make sure that these principles are not lost in the pressure of reorganisation and concerns about funding arrangements.

Health

9.44 The introduction of the National Health Service in 1948 represented a major change for older people. Together with the establishment of a comprehensive structure of sickness and disability benefits, the promise of a free health service did much to alleviate the fear of being ill. The survival of large numbers of people till old age reflects its success.

9.45 People over 75 are the major users of the health services. There are two reasons for this. First, many people who live into old age may develop degenerative diseases. Although in most instances there is no cure, many are helped to lead full lives through ameliorative treatment, but this is of necessity long-term and expensive. Second, elderly people with severe disabilities may be placed in geriatric, mental or other hospitals for longer than is necessary for appropriate investigation and care, and this is wasteful of resources.

9.46   As the number of elderly people in the population has increased, so greater attention has been given to their needs. Doctors have, for example, been encouraged through their remuneration system to offer their patients regular checks on hearing and blood pressure. Under the National Health Service and Community Care Act 1990, health authorities will work with social services departments to provide for people's needs in their homes, primarily through the community nursing service, thus avoiding their admission to hospital for as long as possible. At the same time, the introduction of charges for eye tests and dental care is likely to deter people on limited incomes from seeking help.

9.47   One of the declared aims of the proposed reorganisation of the National Health Service is to reduce waiting lists. While there are great variations throughout the country, people at all ages may have to wait for non-urgent treatment. This may be of more significance to elderly people who have a greater burden of chronic disability, and they may have to wait for long periods for basic treatment such as cataract operations, which means so much in improving their quality of life. Under the reformed service, it is proposed that patients will be able to be treated more quickly if they are willing to travel to hospitals where waiting lists are shorter. This may present problems to frail elderly people. There are questions about the availability and cost of transport, and isolation from family and friends. The desire for increasing speed of treatment and shorter recuperation periods is worrying since elderly people often need more patience and time in diagnosis, treatment and after-care. Also, it is not clear how easily local services can be brought into operation to care for a patient who returns from a distant hospital.

9.48   While in the past a person's age was a strong determining factor in whether or not his or her condition was treated at all, the comment, 'We don't usually do that operation on people of your age,' is less often heard. Dramatic advances in anaesthesia and post-operative care, along with the use of less invasive surgery have resulted in major procedures being carried out on people in their nineties. The decision to proceed may be governed by the gravity of the condition, or by some estimate of the individual's general health. Newer procedures such as transplant surgery are not performed on very elderly people. Perhaps the most significant contribution to improved quality of life in older people has been hip replacements.

9.49 In the case of gravely ill or of very old, incapacitated people the question may arise about the justification for the prolongation of life by medical means, and the possibility of euthanasia. The Board for Social Responsibility's publication *On Dying Well* (CIO, 1975) examines the issues involved here in greater detail. The growth of the hospice movement and a greater understanding of how people can be helped to 'die well' are positive and moral affirmations of individual dignity and human rights. Enhanced nursing techniques and pain control enable many people to remain at home for the major part, if not the whole, of their lives.

9.50 The growth in the private provision of health care mainly in London and the South-East was noted earlier. The Government has recognised that over the last few years more people have been covered by private health insurance as companies have purchased it for their employees. Tax relief on premiums has been given in order to enable people to continue to contribute to insurance schemes after retirement. However, for reasons noted earlier, private health care makes little contribution to the care of chronically ill elderly people—or indeed chronically physically or mentally ill people of any age.

9.51 The other area where growth in private provision has been remarkable is in the provision of nursing homes. These are subject to registration and regulation by the health authorities in the same way as residential homes relate to social services departments.

Education

9.52 Most people of pensionable age left school between the ages of 12 and 14. Eighty per cent of them have no formal qualifications.[23] Yet they were responsible, as taxpayers, for funding the extensive reforms initiated by the Education Act 1944. Most of the current expenditure on education is directed towards schools. Out of a total of £9,000 million, only five per cent is expended on all part-time education. It has been estimated that £1 million is spent on education for older people.[24]

9.53 The wide range of opportunities for continuing learning was outlined in Chapter 7. Older people can take advantage of courses run by the universities, colleges, local authorities or private organisations if they can afford the fees or are, in some way, eligible for grants. Concessions on fees may be made at the discretion of local authorities. Non-vocational courses may be treated differently in this respect from examination courses. The fact remains, though, that currently less than two per cent of retired people are engaged in any formal learning activity. Greater participation would absorb more resources but there could well be benefits in enhancing morale and sometimes in preventing physical deterioration.

Guiding Principles

9.54   Given that services are increasingly to be provided from a variety of sources, how is their quality to be assessed? How do we arrive at the principles which should guide planning?

9.55   First, questions must be asked about how adequately services meet people's needs. How far does provision exceed basic care? Some residential establishments, for example, make sure that people are fed, warm and reasonably clean but do little to provide any stimulus. The morale of elderly people who spend the major part of their days just sitting watching television is quickly undermined. Their physical needs are met, albeit in some places barely, but their mental and spiritual capacities are neglected. As a result, mental confusion can quickly set in.

9.56   Second, services should be provided in an imaginative way which respects people's privacy, their individuality and their relationships. To use residential care as an example again, small clues about the quality of provision are given by whether staff knock on doors before entering, whether there is consultation with the person about how they prefer to be addressed, whether clothes from one person are used for another, and whether necessary intimate questions are put in private or in front of other residents.

9.57   Third, the focus of attention should go beyond the person as an individual, and see them rather as part of a relationship, family or network of friends. Privacy is needed in hospitals, for example, for partners or friends to show affection especially as death approaches. Husbands and wives in residential care who have probably shared a double bed for 50 years should be able to go on doing so if they wish.

9.58   Fourth, there is a need for a spectrum of services and expertise, ranging from neighbourly friendliness and help with shopping to highly skilled staff for assessment, diagnosis, rehabilitation or long-term care. The more that services are local, and able to come to the old person at home, the easier it is to design a support system which meets each individual's needs.

9.59   Finally, there needs to be some choice for people between services. Some people prefer to be with people of their own age, some do not. Some elderly people from certain ethnic groups wish to remain with those with similar culture or religious beliefs. Some elderly people do not like mixed wards in hospitals. Many prefer not to live with their sons or daughters.

Conclusion

9.60   The main thrust of recent welfare policy has been to alter the role of the state in welfare provision. Current proposals for legislation suggest that the state will remain as the main funder of services but that many of these will be obtained increasingly from private and voluntary agencies.

9.61   We remain hesitant however about the capacity of the private and voluntary sector to provide basic services of good quality across the country. Until these sectors have proved that they can undertake such a comprehensive responsibility—particularly in the care of elderly people—we believe it essential that local and national statutory agencies should retain a major responsibility for the provision of services. We also believe it essential that the state continue to monitor the work done by all agencies—whether private, public or voluntary—in order to ensure that what is offered is adequate for people's needs.

Chapter 10

ISSUES FOR THE CHURCH

Introduction

10.1   Our terms of reference asked us to evaluate the Church's own and the wider Christian ministry in the field of ageing, paying particular attention to the contributions and needs of older people in the Church. This chapter looks at two aspects: first, the practical action in which churches engage at local level, and second their national role. Of special importance here is the Church of England's role as a *de facto* employer of many thousands of people. These 'employees' themselves experience loss and change and eventually reach old age: what should our responsibility be? How can churches take account in their own practice of the meaning of ageing to an individual?

10.2   Most of this chapter concerns work with older people. It draws on the letters and papers submitted to the working party,[1] from the experience of working party members, and from the range of parochial and diocesan initiatives described to us. We have heard many stories of skilful and sensitive practice. But we have also heard of work alongside older people where opportunities seem to have been missed. We have therefore been driven to certain conclusions about what ought to happen. It is necessary to spell these out sharply. In coming to these conclusions we are particularly concerned with the Church of England, but our hope is that they may be helpful to other church bodies.

The Local Church

DECIDING ON PRIORITIES

10.3   Within each local church there are different ideas about what the Church—its people, buildings, its life of prayer and witness—is for. They lead to different priorities for work amongst older people. What follows are examples of how four (imaginary) churches understand their ministry and the role of older people. One church

114

may want to try to be a sign of the Kingdom of God by bringing older and younger members together. Implicitly or explicitly its working model is the *family*.

Miss Graham and Mrs Jones met fifty years ago in the confirmation class at St Saviour's. They live in the same street, each with their own house, and neither has children. Church is still a place for meeting people. Over the last few years more families have been coming to the Sunday morning service. Miss Graham and Mrs Jones are delighted that the church is nearly full again. They have helped with the crèche when there haven't been enough volunteers and now they feel like grannies to the whole congregation. Mrs Jones played the piano once when the organist was ill. She taught the congregation an old chorus her mother used to sing and the children invented some actions to go with the chorus. Miss Graham has been babysitting for one couple and they have asked her to be godmother to their new baby which is due next month.

10.4 Other churches are seen by some as a *refuge*, though this need may not always be recognised.

Mr Andrews used to be the churchwarden at St Mary's when there were five curates. Now there is only Father James. Since his wife died, Mr Andrews has been able to get out of the house a bit more. He likes to go up to the church: it is a place where he can sit and remember not only the sad events like his wife's funeral, but the happy ones like his children's christenings and his daughter's wedding. For the last five years he has been going to communion every day. His children would think he was going senile if they knew, but it gives shape to the day. On Thursdays he doesn't go because it is the new service. He doesn't like that. His sight isn't as good as it has been, nor is his memory, and he can remember the old words so easily. Not long ago Father James moved three of the daily eucharists from eleven to seven o'clock in the morning. Now Father James says he would like to use the new service at the seven o'clock. Mr Andrews has always said he would not go and live with his daughter. He wanted to stay at St Mary's right to the end. Now he's not so sure.

10.5 A priority for many churches is *service:*

Mrs Gough can't get out of the house any more. She used to be involved in everything in the village and even now many people drop in to see her so that she still knows what is happening. Mrs Smith comes in every day after she has taken the children to school. She's been doing that ever since Mrs Gough had her fall, three years ago in January. Yesterday Mrs Smith was talking about the new vicar. Apparently he wants to start a scheme to make sure all the old people are visited. Mrs Gough and Mrs Smith had a laugh about that. The vicar doesn't seem to realize just how much visiting is already going on. Mrs Gough said she would tell him when he comes with communion next time. But the women agree that it's a good idea all the same. Some people never see anyone except the doctor and the home help (if they are lucky). And even Mrs Gough could do with some help with the garden. The vicar is talking about starting a youth group. Perhaps they could do something with the front hedge.

10.6   Finally, there are churches for which the priority is *prophetic action:*

Mr John hasn't been to church since he arrived in Britain as a young man. He left all that to his wife. She seemed to cope better than him with being the only black family in the place. Now he's on his own and finding it difficult to get about. Last month they closed the café where he used to meet his friends. They say that a club is opening at the church down the street—every lunchtime during the week. They say that the church is building new small houses for old people and if you go to the club you can go on the list. Mr John isn't sure. They will want him to go to church. They say it's not true. And anyway it's not so bad now: the church has a black pastor. Perhaps next week he'll try it out.

FROM GENERATION TO GENERATION

10.7   A common feature of all these examples is an understanding of the local church as an all-age community. Here links are sought and welcomed—or at least should be welcomed—between people of all ages. Such an idea is the main theme in the Board of Education's report on all-age worship *Children in the Way* (NS/CHP) and its follow-up publication *Leaves on the Tree* (NS/CHP). *Children in the Way* begins with this invitation:

Imagine a church congregation in which men and women, girls and boys, young and old, share together to worship God, to learn from one another about their faith, to pray together about their mutual concerns and joys, to serve those in need and to reach out with the Gospel to those in the community who are outside the Church. Whenever possible, the members are not separated into groups according to age or sex but are together. At times, of course, there *are* activities for parents and very young children, a club for lively junior age children, a group for adolescents and study sessions for adults. But the first instinct of this Church is to say 'What can we *all* do?' This is the vision of the authors of this report. Although we recognise that there may be many steps along the way before some parishes can achieve the reality, we ask you to share in this vision.

10.8   Reading *Children in the Way* with older people in mind is a curious experience. Again and again what the report says about children is of great importance for elderly people as well. For example this is the comment on the double meaning in the title.

> We want children to come 'into the way of faith' with adults. We want adults to overcome any feelings that children are merely 'in the way'. So often the Church may appear to be indifferent to the needs of children and, sadly, some adults are unaware of the contribution which children can make to the life of the Church.

The same could be said for the way elderly people are sometimes perceived.

10.9   The report also comments:

> In our thinking, age differences are less important than a shared Christian calling to walk in the way of Christ. For us children are important; people with needs to be met and a contribution to make to the life of the Church. This view may not be shared by all Church members or congregations. Some accept and welcome the children in their own right, some are merely tolerant, some are sentimental in their attitude towards them and some see children as of no importance.

and

> Our conviction is simple. If children are to continue in the way of faith, if they are to continue on the path to which the Church welcomed them at baptism, then they must be aided and supported by the adult fellow-Christians who are also on that journey and must be acknowledged as those who sometimes lead the way. We invite you to join us in searching for new strategies and models for Christian education in parishes, in order that both adults and children may journey together in the way of Christ, growing into his full stature and serving his world.

10.10   Every local church has the potential to be a community of different generations. There is an important sense in which Christians do not choose each other. They often find themselves worshipping with people of all ages, backgrounds and ethnic origins. The riches and tensions that come from being interdependent, and the experience of growth and change which were outlined in Part II of this report are lived out day by day in local churches.

10.11   A word is needed about the tensions. First, it has to be recognised that many church communities are themselves ageing, and experience collectively the questions about the future which an individual faces. They may ask: 'Who will keep our church going when this generation of worshippers has died?' or 'If we abandon evensong because so few people are coming, will it be the thin end of the wedge?' Sometimes these questions lead to despair or a sense of failure. Sometimes they lead to a neglect of those people who do actually come in order to try to bring in a new younger congregation. This is mainly true of established mainstream denominations where figures show that the number of young committed members is declining. The black-led churches, the house church movement and some churches within the evangelical tradition are growing steadily.

10.12 A second tension concerns the conflicts that can arise between generations within a church. Chapters 2 and 9 mentioned the issue of 'intergenerational equity' which has arisen in the USA, where some middle-aged groups are now accusing elderly people of taking more than their 'fair share' of the nation's resources. A similar polarisation can take place in churches. The Sunday School needs storage space for its material in the church hall cupboards, but the extra chairs for the elderly people's luncheon club also have to be stored somewhere. Or the church council spends hours debating whether the children in the parent and toddlers' group should be allowed to play with sand (which they love but which damages the wood blocks on the floor). Somehow the discussion begins to sound more and more critical of the children themselves. At the same time the rota for transporting elderly people to church has broken down and the task is falling on one or two people. Both discussions easily turn into a blaming session, with an unspoken assumption in the air that all would be well if everyone were adult and able-bodied. Another common tension is that of older people not wanting to let go of their role on committees or as office-holders, leaving younger people feeling excluded.

10.13 Most churches face conflicts like these from time to time. What is certain however is that many congregations have managed to stay with the conflicts and have in the end gained much through links across the generations. One example of this comes from Kent:

> The Parish of Whitstable is typical of many of our seaside parishes in Kent, with a high proportion of elderly and retired parishioners. The church here seeks to exercise a pastoral ministry to them while recognising that they have a real contribution to make in their own right. Without their time, experience and insight the church would be impoverished.
>
> In our church services we have attempted for many years to seek a healthy balance between *stability* and *change*: between traditional and modern music

118

and hymns, and between Prayer Book and Alternative Service Book. Although there are inevitable compromises to be made, this policy coupled with good communication has produced an atmosphere in which young and old alike feel a sense of belonging and worth.

We have a large number of housebound or semi-housebound parishioners whose active, or rather *physically* active role in church life has come to an end. In the All Saints district alone some 120 church members receive their communion regularly either in their own homes or in one of the retirement homes through the ministry of the clergy, readers and authorised lay people.

For those who have been regular worshipping members in the past, this contact with their local church and its activities is obviously extremely important, but it is only part of the story. They also have a need to contribute. Here in Whitstable we felt that perhaps the best way of achieving this would be through the activity of prayer. Thus, the 'Fellowship of Prayer' came into being.

Since its beginning in 1983, the Fellowship of Prayer has grown and now has some 150 members. Six times a year they receive a booklet containing meditations, prayers and suggested topics for intercession. These are intended to supplement but certainly not replace the member's own pattern of prayer.

In this way the Fellowship attempts to meet the needs of the Church by having a large body of informed people united in prayer, and of the individual who is kept in touch with the local and world-wide concerns of the Church and perhaps equally important with each other through the list of members published in each issue. As one member put it: 'I feel I meet old friends each week.' Some members have also offered to intercede in cases of emergency, in which case they are contacted by telephone.

We realise that it is impossible to generalise. People vary both in their needs and in their mental and physical capacities, and what works in one parish may not bear fruit in another, but we trust our experience may be of help to others.[2]

CARING FOR THE CARERS

10.14   Elsewhere in this report we describe changing family patterns, and the increased mobility and longer life expectancy which are affecting our ability to care for each other. We point to the high number of people caring for dependent relatives, and the frequently inadequate support given to them. We also argue that the current emphasis on the individual and the consumer can have the effect of undervaluing those human activities which are not to do with the market and profit.

10.15   The Christian tradition shows that the giving and receiving of care is at the heart of being human. Caring for a dependent person can be immensely rewarding, and so can the experience of learning to accept care. Duty to father and mother, to child, neighbours and strangers is a part of our calling. But the centrality of care should not blind us to the long-term stress it can cause, or free us from the responsibility to share its demands. Churches particularly need to beware of romanticising care and taking for granted the great sacrifices that many make.

10.16   At present a great deal of loving painstaking care is offered by families. Much of it is invisible. Within the smallest church congregation there will probably be people who are spending hour after hour, largely unnoticed, caring for dependent older relatives. Often they may be elderly themselves. Often they will be experiencing great stress and loneliness. Within every neighbourhood there is also an 'absent congregation'—people who would like to come to church but are prevented by their own disability or by their reluctance to leave their dependent relative unattended.

10.17   The Church has several roles here. First, it can assert that carers should not have to do everything single-handed. A carer's own needs are crucial, and it is entirely proper to expect some assistance from outside. It is particularly important for churches to affirm this, because the legacy of the Victorian Christian tradition has meant that free self-giving has often been distorted into subservience, guilt and unexpressed anger. Carers have needs and these must be recognised. Second, churches can offer practical help. Often a little assistance, offered sensitively and at the right time, can transform a carer's life. Indeed it can make the difference between his or her keeping going or being stretched to breaking point. Much can be learned from the hospice movement, which has opened up new ways of sharing the care and responsibility for a gravely ill or dying person, and has freed carers to have occasional breaks.

VALUING THE SPIRITUAL JOURNEY

10.18   As was mentioned in Chapter 1, many of the older people who wrote to us stressed the spiritual dimension of ageing. They said that clergy were sometimes more willing to offer a careful ministry of preaching, teaching and pastoral care to young people than to old, and that their own needs were disregarded. They also felt sometimes that what they had to offer to the life of the Church was not being understood and valued.

10.19   What is essential is a greater honesty about both the spiritual needs and the riches associated with growing older. The spiritual riches and discernment of old age can be seen dramatically in the lives of people like Catherine Booth of the Salvation Army, John Wesley, who ordained ministers for America at the age of 81, and Pope John XXIII who called the Second Vatican Council at 78 years of age. For many people an awareness of the presence of God through their lives will help them to make some sense of ageing and dying. But religious belief does not necessarily mean that there will be emotional adjustment to growing old. Nor does it necessarily lead to a strong sense of personal worth. For some growing older is accompanied by feelings of isolation and uncertainty about God, compounded by a sense that these uncertainties are shameful and cannot be admitted.

10.20   To talk only about a serene old age can therefore be as one-sided as to talk only about deterioration. Indeed, it is now established that the incidence of depression among the older age group is higher than within the population as a whole. Sadly it often goes unnoticed. We do people an injustice if it is assumed that because they are old and are coming to church every Sunday they no longer want to talk about their faith. As one man in his seventies said:

> You can't tell the Vicar that you get stuck with your prayers at my age. You're supposed to know it all, aren't you?

Another letter sent to us included this comment:

> It is no good ignoring the death that awaits us all. The Church cannot ignore the great vast question mark that looms before all old people. For the young it may be sufficient to say 'God is with us. The Kingdom of God is here and now' (although I have known young people terrified by the thought of death). But when so many of one's loved ones and friends have died, how can we shelve death and what comes after as irrelevant to our life here and now? If the Church fails in its duty to give real comfort and show the way to Jesus, there will be little hope for those involved when they face that leap in the dark. Give physical comfort yes, but do not neglect the spiritual comfort.[3]

Some people may wish to be offered carefully structured spiritual direction. Others need above all to be listened to, and shown warmth and confidence. One writer to us summed up the matter:

> Above all, a sensitive encouragement is essential. I feel that we should be far more skilled than we are at helping people at the end of their lives feel good about their lives, to feel that life has had worth.[4]

RITES OF PASSAGE

10.21   The Church has always been closely involved with the process of ageing. It accompanies people through 'life events' through its ministry at times of birth, marriage and death. All these things are part of ageing—they mean new commitments, changes in family patterns, loss and growth. For centuries people have chosen to celebrate and mark the most important moments of life within a religious framework.

10.22   The development of a society where fewer people go to church regularly has not reduced the importance of these rites of passage. Indeed it seems to be fundamental to human beings to find public ways of marking changes in an individual's life. Societies which neglect or try to abandon their formal processes of celebration and mourning are likely to be impoverished and to manage the making and breaking of bonds less successfully than others. As individuals and as groups we need to celebrate the birth of a child, make public the commitment of two adults to each other, and mourn someone who has died.

10.23   An example of this was the public response to the disasters that occurred during late 1988 and early 1989. The air disasters at Lockerbie and on the M1, and the football tragedy at Hillsborough were all events where communities experienced a completely unexpected loss. In the days that followed people created their own holy places. The pitch at Anfield became a shrine of scarves and flowers. Churches gave practical help and, more important, planned sensitive memorial services and funerals which brought bereaved people together. Through the expression of Christian hope and through symbol, story and song, they were able to offer something that no secular institution could.

10.24   The same can be said of the thousands of less visible rites of passage which take place in churches week by week—baptisms, marriages, funerals. It is encouraging that people continue to seek these events in great number. Churches have the opportunity to take these responsibilities seriously and to offer as imaginative and committed a contact as possible.

10.25   Again new ways are being discovered of reaching people at times of special need. One church in Essex holds a service twice a year for the relatives of all those bereaved in the last six months. The church is always packed and the names of those who have died are read out quietly. The service is a way of showing relatives that the church goes on being interested in them and wanting to support them long beyond the actual funeral. Some churches also now invite couples celebrating say fifty years of marriage to come together for an act of thanksgiving.

DEATH AND HEAVEN

10.26   For all of us there is the question of what happens when the ageing process is over. For many people in the second half of life ageing is bound up with loss. There is the slow but steady loss of physical powers, status, friends and partners and final loss of life itself. There are also the unexpected bereavements that occur throughout life— the death of a young vital friend, a miscarriage, sudden redundancy or disabling illness. For all the gains, of grandchildren perhaps, and of self-acceptance, the main experience may be of diminishment. How are we to understand such things?

10.27   A Christian approach to ageing emphasises the confidence that, even in situations of extreme difficulty, there is hope and the possibility of growth and change. The human spirit can stay alive through the most painful and constricting of situations. This hope is no glib optimism; rather a knowledge that suffering has been transformed through Christ's death and resurrection.

10.28   This Christian understanding of resurrection changes utterly our attitude to loss and finally to death. A great challenge for the Church in the late twentieth century is to find ways of interpreting what this resurrection means. For it is clear that many of the images which earlier generations had—those of angels and archangels, heaven and hell, Hades, the Elysian Fields, even of Valhalla (the hall of the slain in Viking mythology)—have largely left modern consciousness. Heaven and the final judgement have ceased to be real for many. As clergy know from their ministry of funerals, the old three-decker understanding of the universe—of heaven, earth and hell—has gone. There has been a profound change in the human psyche, and the journey from womb to brain death is widely believed to be the whole story of humanity.

10.29   It has become almost impossible to find a language with which to talk about death and what lies beyond. And so the temptation is not to talk about death at all, and to fear every sign of it that we see in our daily lives. Christians have many questions and uncertainties. But we can be confident of God's love beyond the grave, and so we can risk using bolder language and more vibrant images. As St Paul put it: 'I reckon that the sufferings we now endure bear no comparison with the splendour that is in store for us.'

10.30   It may be that one of the tasks of the Church now is to live in a way which shows not just how God is present in the ordinariness of everyday life, but also that there are splendours to come. As one speaker on 'Thought for the Day' put it: 'Some theologians say we must accept the state of the twentieth century mind and discover our motivation and morality and our hope without a supernatural backdrop. But I believe that we should rebuild the eternal city, reopen our contemporary mind to a vision of the heavenly places, re-educate our imagination to the possibility of God's dimension. Perhaps our vision will not be just like the Book of Revelation, but that is no reason to close the shutter on the truth we sense but do not see. If, rather than the dead end of slipping quietly behind the crematorium curtain, we believed we entered the halls of God's glory, it would transform so much in our lives; the way we tackle terminal illness, the way we decide our values, the goals we set and the way we treat each other.'[5]

USING BUILDINGS CREATIVELY

10.31   Many churches own buildings which have great potential but are under-used. Sometimes redundant churches can be adapted in most imaginative ways. For example:

> For fifteen years a church in central York has been used as a day centre for elderly people. St Sampson's in York was made redundant in 1968, having outlived its usefulness as a parish church. For several years it remained locked and neglected while many schemes were proposed for its use. Finally money was raised for it to be turned into a centre for elderly

people. The architects were asked to keep the original layout of the church as far as possible; kitchen, warden's room, lavatories were created. The former sanctuary became a small chapel at the east end with a quiet room for reading adjoining it. Today average attendance is about 1500, with numerous activities, meals and opportunities for making friends. The atmosphere is relaxed, informal, busy. Volunteers and paid staff offer informal care at its best for those who have no close family or friends. The staff do not seek to do everything—they believe for example that it is their task to work with those who are mobile enough to get to the centre, and are trying to do that well.

The Church Urban Fund is also helping fund a number of projects. In Blackburn the conversion of a church interior in 1990 is providing facilities for a range of services, especially for old people living alone, young families and ethnic minorities. The Northwood parish hall in Stoke-on-Trent is being used as a meeting place for confused elderly people; with Church Urban Fund money, two additional rooms are to be built in order to make space for chiropody and for practical activities such as hairdressing and counselling. In Harehill, Leeds, local churches have bought a shop on the High Street, and are running a café called 'Meeting Point' for young people and elderly people.

10.32   Despite some progress, most churches make little or no practical provision for the difficulties and disabilities that may accompany old age. Sometimes the desire to save money or to preserve a building intact takes precedence over the needs of people wishing to use the building. A church that has no lavatories within easy reach, where the acoustics are poor and there is no wheelchair access, is conveying strong messages about the welcome it really wants to extend to older people.

The Church's National Role

CHALLENGING AGEISM

10.33   Chapter 6 argued that negative attitudes to ageing are a feature of society. They are also a feature of the Church. As one letter said: 'It seems to me that the Church in Britain quite simply reflects the same attitudes to old age and older people as the society in which it is set. It has allowed "the world" to squeeze it into its mould, and has failed to challenge the myths and the underlying fear of age and death. . . .'[6]

10.34 Examples of how the Church has reinforced a negative view of ageing are easy to find. A radio Lent course on church growth and evangelism was largely devoted to how young people and families with children might be recruited, and virtually ignored older people, despite their number. The implication was that young people are the important people, needed for the future, and that older people have had their day.

10.35 There is usually much greater emphasis in diocesan appointments on work with children and young people. Few dioceses have an older people's committee or an older people's officer, and there is often little effort made to represent their interests or to explore innovative ministry with them. Language used in church life and documents often reflects negative attitudes. As Chapter 6 noted, small asides like 'The old people here are all so traditional', 'They need a coffee club or outing' and 'Isn't he rather past it to be a churchwarden?' may mask much prejudice. One diocesan study pack was particularly blatant. Designed to encourage parish reflection before the Lambeth Conference in 1988 it stated confidently: 'All Christians without exception, whether they are lay or ordained, women or men, old or young, have a common vocation. All are called to ministry.' But in the same pack, readers were asked to respond to the following question:

'What kind of body would best describe your church?

Is it:

Geriatric?	Middle aged?
Legless?	Functioning with difficulty?
Youthful?	Dispirited?
Paralysed?	All mouth?
Growing?	Mature?
Decapitated?	Something else?

'Geriatric' and 'middle aged' are clearly used pejoratively, and are insulting to old people.

10.36 Often churches plan events for older people without discovering their ideas on what is needed or what they would enjoy. They should be allowed to plan and participate in such events. For example, it is relatively easy to organise a carol service in the local residential home. But the lack of consultation and collaboration with the people who live there undervalues them by denying their contribution.

10.37   How can ageism be challenged? First, it is important to own up to the complex dimension which lies behind ageism—our own fear of dying and of death. Older people show us what we will become; that so many current images of old age involve poverty, ill health and immobility, inevitably means that old people become a warning of what we fear awaits us. Christians have to be careful not to claim too much, and yet the belief in the infinite importance of every person and the Christian hope of eternal life in which God's love continues to be experienced beyond death challenge any attitude which sees death as the ultimate evil.

10.38   Second, the Church is in a strong position to question some of the accepted norms of society. Attitudes towards older people in industrialised societies have been distorted by the linking of status with paid employment. Those who are not carrying out productive labour are seen as less valuable members of society. It is not of course retired people alone who are diminished by this attitude. Studies of young unemployed people, middle-aged people suddenly made redundant, and indeed parents remaining at home to care for their children, all show that the experience of being without paid employment can be one of exclusion from the mainstream of society. But older people are particularly vulnerable to being set on one side.

10.39   Third, the Church needs to examine its own strategy about worship and evangelism. A Church Army paper on evangelism commenting on the common assumption that young people should be of prime importance in designing worship, emphasises the value of the familiar: ' "Songs of Praise" is well loved and reaches a wide audience and its hymns can open up memories of faith, lost or hidden. Elderly people of the present generation were brought up in what was clearly a Christian country with teaching in school and regular church attendance. Tapping those memories is one place to begin our work.'[7] We hope that older people will play a part in the new energy and reflection released during the Decade of Evangelism.

COMMENTING ON PUBLIC POLICY

10.40   Chapter 9 considered the current debate about welfare services and suggested a number of principles. The Church has a duty to scrutinise government policy—whichever party is in power—and try to ensure that services develop in ways which do not put frail and vulnerable people at a disadvantage or strengthen the divisions that already exist.

10.41   One of the most worrying features of some developments in social policy is the increasing emphasis on the individual. For all their flaws and shortcomings it has been the strength of the National Health Service and the other provisions of the welfare state to encourage a sense of responsibility across the community. Behind many of the reforms implemented in the 1940s was an important principle—that of solidarity with others whom one would almost certainly never meet personally but whose needs merited support from the whole Church. The intergenerational connection was particularly important. Family allowance (now called child benefit) was seen as a way of the whole community helping with the cost of bringing up children. Pension payments were intended not only as contributions to an individual's pension but also as a sharing of the costs of supporting all old people.

10.42   The risk is that some current policies will erode this principle of interdependence and that it will be hard to recover. In a world of individualism it is easy to drive wedges between generations and to set up battles for resources. This is already beginning to take place in the United States.

ENCOURAGING LOCAL POLICIES AND PROVISION

10.43   A further issue for churches concerns their involvement in running welfare services. It is likely that over the next twenty years churches will be asked by local authorities to become more involved in practical social care. This may mean taking on relatively small–scale enterprises, such as managing and running playgroups for parents and toddlers, or luncheon clubs for elderly people. But the signs are that they may well be asked to accept much more costly and ambitious work, such as managing hospices or residential care.

10.44   As Chapter 9 argued, this shift in expectations of what the voluntary organisations and churches should do has come about partly because of the breakdown of consensus about the welfare state. The General Synod in 1987 was clear that the state ought to retain a major responsibility for funding and providing basic services. All the indications are that the 'mixed economy of welfare', ie, a partnership between public bodies such as local authorities, voluntary agencies and the private sector, is here to stay.

10.45 Complex issues are involved here and careful judgements are needed about the proper role of churches in social care. Churches have often pioneered compassionate work with those in need and new forms emerge all the time. For example, the community projects developing up and down the country, many of them supported by the Church Urban Fund, are a 1980s version of the robust work carried out by the Church of England's 'moral welfare' workers of the 1930s and 1940s. But we stress our hesitation about the ability of voluntary or indeed private agencies to provide large-scale services of quality across the country. In our view churches should do all they can to support new initiatives but be cautious about necessarily managing them.

RESPONDING TO TRAINING NEEDS

10.46 Another step for the Church is to examine the training lay people and clergy receive in working with older people. Many issues dealt with in this report are already referred to in different parts of the pastoral studies programmes of theological colleges. Rites of passage, for example, care of elderly people, all-age worship, and stages of faith are all likely to be discussed at some time.

10.47 Our own studies in the preparation of this report have made us aware that the subject of ageing could be a good candidate for the integrative approach to theological studies which is now being widely advocated. Biblical, doctrinal, liturgical, ethical and pastoral studies are all involved, as well as inter-disciplinary work between theology and the psychological and sociological human sciences. We therefore suggest that those responsible for theological training for clergy take this possibility seriously.

10.48 A particular concern of this report is to combat ageism. There is reason to believe that this prejudice about the value of elderly people (for example when measuring the quality of a congregation's life) is shared by ordinands, clergy and younger lay people. The prejudice of ageism in their own attitudes needs to be confronted by ordinands as ruthlessly as does that of racism and sexism. It is important that they encounter elderly people in the course of their training, and not simply sick elderly people to whom they are of course called to minister. They need also to have seen the central role strong and wise elderly persons can play in the Christian community. Elderly people can show others much about prayer and spirituality, courage and freshness.

10.49 Increasing recognition is now being given to enabling ordinands to help themselves and others to pray. We suggest that those responsible for such programmes pay particular attention to helping people to pray at the transitions of their lives, and especially at crucial periods in later life, e.g., retirement, bereavement, increasing infirmity or disability. Clergy need to be ready to help such people see their prayer life as an integral part of the life of the Christian community if they are housebound. Indeed housebound people may have a special ministry of prayer precisely because of their detachment from the rush and bustle of life. As Maggie Kuhn, leader of the Gray Panthers in the USA, puts it: 'It might just be one of God's surprises for us that He may use those closest to death, nearer to the other life, to show the Church how to break with self-centred purposes and goals and work to the good of all and serve God.'[8]

10.50 Perhaps most important will be helping ordinands and clergy (in the course of Continuing Ministerial Education) come to terms with their own ageing, and thus ultimately with their own mortality. If they have been able to do this, they will be better able to help others in their ageing.

IMPROVING EMPLOYMENT PRACTICES

10.51 Churches in this country employ directly or indirectly many thousands of people. Their jobs range from full-time work where a life-long commitment to church employment has been made (such as clergy), to short-term and part-time work (such as workers employed for a few months to run a summer playscheme based in a church). Between these two poles lies a variety of occupations. Musicans, parish secretaries, church hall caretakers, community workers and youth workers are but a few. It was not the task of the working party to look in detail at these different patterns of employment. Some work has already been done, such as a Board of Education report on *Sector Ministries* and a current working party of the Advisory Council for the Church's Ministry. However, it did seem essential to consider how the themes of this report might influence the Church of England's employment practice. Here we suggest four areas of particular importance.

Provision for housing and income maintenance

10.52 Some historical background is helpful. Church of England clergy have always been self-employed in law. The 'living' was literally that, a permanent agreement between a clergyman and a parish which gave some element, even if small, of financial security. There is now greater awareness that the relatively low pay of clergy combined with usually many years in tied accommodation can lead to real difficulties. In the last few decades pension and retirement schemes have been introduced and these represent steps towards a more centralised policy. Thought has been given to the housing needs of retired clergy and some provision made. Standardisation of clergy salaries has been operating for many years now. All these are welcome steps towards recognising that confidence about housing and about income is important for clergy, as indeed it is for people at all ages and especially in old age.

Valuing the lay contribution

10.53   There is no doubt however that the needs of clergy have been taken more seriously than those of lay people employed by the Church. Lay people who have come from secular agencies are often amazed at the lack of priority given to job descriptions, contracts, and careful interviewing techniques. Many have questioned the common assumption that those matters are unimportant and 'worldly' and have used their experience to show that close attention to structures is a sign of the Church's commitment to the post and the person appointed. We welcome the growing interest in defining job boundaries in both clergy and lay posts.

Identifying and managing stress

10.54   In the last few years the teaching, medical, social work and nursing professions and the police service have all paid more attention than before to stress levels among their workers. The apparent need to maintain a strong exterior and to deny feelings of sadness, anger and powerlessness, can sometimes build up to the point where the person can no longer work effectively. Clergy and lay people working for the Church frequently share such pressures. In their work they encounter the depths of pain, sadness and anxiety. For them there are often no clear boundaries between the personal and public dimensions of life. They may have to live with demands to be all things to all people, and with the tension of being expected to be peacemaker at the same time as leader. Doing the job day by day is both a privilege and a responsibility.

10.55   Earlier chapters have suggested that stress, loss and conflict are all part of life and are not to be avoided at all costs. Yet the risks of overwork and lack of support can be great in a church culture which tends to emphasise action rather than contemplation. So it is good that the needs for greater support and training throughout working life are beginning to be recognised by the Church of England. Most dioceses now offer clergy a chance to review their work and development once a year, and encourage the use of work consultants especially in team ministries.

Encouraging preparation for retirement

10.56   This report has argued that retirement can be experienced both as one of the greatest losses in life, and an event which opens up many new possibilities. For clergy the concept of retirement is likely to raise many problems. It can be difficult to hold together a commitment to a whole lifetime in the ordained ministry with the sense of not being immediately needed. Many clergy and their partners flourish in parish situations where they are in some sense the pivot. They find their identity through close involvement with a particular community and derive deep fulfilment from their ministry of accompanying people at points of change and crisis. The losses that retirement involves can therefore be particularly acute.

10.57   One important way of facing up to these changes is to join with others in talking about them in advance. Pre-retirement courses, now a well-established feature of the secular world, are becoming much more common within the Church. At least half the dioceses have run pre-retirement courses since 1987, and these courses cover topics such as pensions, housing and health. The most valuable courses are likely to be those where there is a strong emphasis on psychological and spiritual aspects and where the group meets for five or six days over as many weeks. For example the Institute of Christian Studies in London runs courses in co-operation with the Christian Council on Ageing. Clergy and their partners are encouraged to explore in depth their hopes and fears surrounding retirement. Over several weeks they reflect on how the changes in their public ministry may affect their interior life, their relationships and their sense of themselves in the world. The aim is to help the participants recognise that they are likely to experience retirement both as bereavement and as gain.

LEARNING FROM RELIGIOUS COMMUNITIES

10.58   Finally it has been put to us that the Church has much to learn about ageing from a small but significant group within it—the religious communities. Demographic trends and changed attitudes to lifetime commitment within the religious life have meant that many religious communities have had to face their own ageing and to discern new roles. They have had to reappraise radically their strategy, and consider how to use their resources of buildings, people and money. They have learnt to live with the painful tension of honouring the needs of their own members, and of being a strong Christian presence in the world.

10.59   Often the changes have involved the letting go of buildings, and with them the letting go of a certain status. We give three examples. First, a well-established men's community, famous as a place for retreat and spiritual direction, sells off its spacious premises to move into a much smaller house in the next county. Second, the mother house of a women's order established a century ago parts company with its imposing Victorian structure with cloisters, echoing corridor and enormous garden. The new convent is purpose-built within the grounds and is paid for by adapting the mother house into luxurious housing for business people and their families. Third, an Anglican women's contemplative order offers a diocese the use of a house belonging to the community. The house has a fine chapel and accommodation for 14 people, but the community cannot afford to run it any longer.

10.60   There are two main reasons for these changes in religious communities. The first is that most religious communities now have many more elderly sisters and brothers needing specialised nursing care. Orders increasingly have to use younger able-bodied members to offer this care. They may also need to use secular agency nurses— thereby adding to the cost of running the community. The second reason is the reduction in the number of people entering the religious life. Orders have always relied on young people as their source of recruitment and renewal. In the Roman Catholic Church in the past, many families were keen to send a daughter to the convent and a son to the priesthood, but this tradition is vanishing with fewer practising Catholics and smaller families. Women in all church traditions, whether married or unmarried, now have greater scope for service without the need to join a religious order. Young people can for example consider overseas aid programmes such as Voluntary Service Overseas or work in this country with Community Service Volunteers. The special long-term commitment that the religious life offers is less compelling. It is also the case that orders are more and more cautious about whom they will admit. A newcomer may well be in his or her late twenties or older, have a profession and be a wage-earner. The question of motivation has to be fully and responsibly explored. Is there true vocation, or is this a lonely immature person who, through fear of living alone, yearns for the apparent security of the religious life?

10.61   Given these radical shifts in demography and recruitment, religious communities have begun to pay increasing attention to the impact of an ageing population and shrinking numbers. They are much more aware of how difficult the concept of 'retirement' can be for people who have made a life commitment to a particular form of ministry. Moving from full-time employment in education, hospital, parish and mission work to a slower rhythm of life can lead to sharp physical and mental decline. Often the emphasis on being continually occupied and emotionally invulnerable, the ethos in some communities, can expose feelings of worthlessness and the dread of being a burden on anyone else when life is no longer so active.

10.62   More has also been done to explore concrete ways in which religious communities can prepare their members for old age and for new forms of ministry. The Association of Senior Religious was founded in 1974 within the Roman Catholic Church, and now has members from men's orders and Church of England orders. Its aim is to explore and develop together the contribution of the older religious to the apostolic mission of the church today. One of the Association's discoveries was that the foundation statutes of religious communities make little mention of the needs of retired and elderly people, and that such guidelines as there were tended to be highly general. One constitution, for example, stated that, 'Each sister, aware that retirement is a time for personal growth and continued participation in the life and mission of the community, will prepare herself for this period, and the community will assist her in this preparation.' No indication was given however about how this might happen.

10.63   Finally, there has been a gradual shedding of the responsibility for running large institutions. This has never been achieved without conflict and pain and often a deep sense of loss, but often new energies have been liberated. It is not now uncommon to find in inner cities and outer estates a small house occupied by three or four religious. One or more may have full-time or part-time employment locally, one may be a pensioner, their state pension adding to the common purse. The life is one of shared simplicity and humility—with a daily office, the discipline of community rule, and a desire to affirm others. Such a microcosm of the larger religious community can provide a place of welcome in our fragmented stressful cities. Local people, especially perhaps those who are lonely and confused, are drawn in to enjoy hospitality, and are nourished by a spirituality which is focused on quietly 'being' rather than energetically 'doing'. All this is a dramatic reversal of half a century ago when religious communities were endowed with great resources and were involved in residential care, hospitals and schools. The philosophy of 'care in the community', with small households replacing the large institution, is paralleled by this paring down of religious communities into local community-based units. Religious communities have adapted to change and ageing with an imaginative risk-taking and sense of hope which has much to offer the rest of the Church and secular society.

Chapter 11

SUMMARY OF FINDINGS

11.1 The working party was asked to do three things. First, we were required to consider demographic trends, social policy questions and theories of ageing. In doing this we found many misunderstandings about ageing. In particular the numbers of old people are frequently exaggerated, and their health and fitness underestimated.

11.2 Second, the working party was asked to evaluate the Church's own ministry towards older people. We found many stories of love, service and concern, but also examples of contributions and needs of older people being ignored.

11.3 Third, we were asked to provide a critical theological approach to the trends, policies and theories outlined above. Here we drew on biblical material and other Christian resources, and reflected on the life of faith. In considering the notions of dependence and independence from a Christian point of view it became evident that every human life, all human relationships and a person's relationship with God contain both dependence and independence.

11.4 The following sections provide a summary of the key findings of the working party. We outline those challenges to policy-makers which are presented by major social trends. We examine what those trends might mean for the Church, especially how it supports people through their ageing and how it responds to their changing physical, emotional and spiritual needs. We conclude by restating the principles which we believe should inform a Christian approach to ageing.

Challenges to Policy-Makers

11.5 We welcome the new interest in ageing across the disciplines. There is a growing body of research which addresses the needs of older people and looks at old age in the context of the whole lifespan.

11.6 Much careful and imaginative work with older people is done by medical, social services and residential care staffs. We recognise and affirm the commitment that many of them make to the well-being of older people. It is however worrying that the quality and availability of services for elderly people is so variable across the country. Despite attempts to make improvements, many people live out their old age in below-standard housing, on very low incomes, and with little professional support. We know too that some elderly people—often those who are weakest—experience emotional and physical abuse and this is deeply disturbing.

11.7 It is good that in the 1980s much progress was made on articulating the rights of children. It is now time to look at the other end of the lifespan and consider the rights of older people.

11.8 The next few years will see major changes in the way health and welfare services are organised. It is too early to know what the long-term effects will be, but it is certain that the quality of life of older people will be affected by the adequacy of the new schemes, and the resources committed to them. We have recognised that the 'mixed economy of welfare' in the public, private and voluntary sectors is here to stay, and welcome the increasing emphasis being made on the voluntary sector. In our view it is essential, however, that basic services continue to be funded through taxation and provided nationwide. To use the Confederation of British Industry's phrase, we need 'initiatives beyond charity'. Without a coherent state-monitored and state-provided framework of services, the chances of all people receiving the good quality health and social care that they need throughout their lives will be much reduced.

11.9 This report has argued that the later years of life can be years of great fulfilment. Pre-retirement education and continuing access to education make a significant contribution here and should be more widely available. Parliament and employers need to address the question of more flexible statutory ages for retirement from paid employment.

11.10 Carers need to be affirmed and supported. Caring for a dependent relative can be very rewarding but the personal price is often high. Caring may disrupt careers, detract from other relationships and lead people into poverty. The role of carers has been given more attention in recent years, but they need adequate financial and emotional support and help not only from professionals, but from the wider community.

137

11.11   Policy-makers and planners need to be aware of the importance of gender issues in old age. At present there are significantly more very elderly women than men. Although roles may well change in the years ahead the majority of those caring for dependent relatives at present are women.

11.12   In the next twenty years a growing number of members of minority ethnic groups will reach old age. In the past the special needs of elderly black people have often been neglected by welfare agencies who accepted the stereotype of strong and supportive black communities. Progress is being made to make welfare services more sensitive to elderly black people. This should be encouraged and developed.

11.13   Finally, policy-makers should emphasise the connection between the generations. It is likely that in the years ahead there will be growing competition between groups for scarce resources. Great efforts need to be made to build a sense of shared responsibility of one generation for another. This is a matter for governments and political parties, not simply individuals and families.

Opportunities for the Churches

11.14   In accompanying people of all ages through the rites of passage, churches have a rich opportunity to respond to the desire of many to recognise God's presence in their lives.

11.15   Churches need to recognise the centrality of prayer and spirituality in their work with all age groups. The prayer of older people can be a special contribution.

11.16   Churches need to affirm the value of older people to the whole life of the Church—in its worship, work and witness. The Church is an all-age community, where each stage of faith has its own authority.

11.17   The Church of England has very mixed responses to ageing and to old age in particular. It both idolises and dismisses old people, and this is reflected in the policies it advocates and adopts. For example, the Church talks positively about caring but often fails to recognise the burden which this can impose on family members and the resentment which may follow. It also frequently adopts negative attitudes to older people. It is important that the Church begins to recognise and address its own ageism.

11.18   The years 1991 to 2000 have been named the Decade of Evangelism. It is likely that the focus of this will be on younger people. Older people may however have as much need for sensitive evangelistic contact as younger people, and may have as much to give in bringing the Gospel to others.

11.19   Churches need a more systematic approach to older people in congregations. Dioceses could consider setting up special interest groups on ageing to look at local needs and responses. Training needs of lay people and clergy should be addressed in this context.

11.20   In their stewardship of buildings, and design of worship, churches should pay special attention to matters such as access for people with disabilities, loop systems for people with hearing difficulties, and easily accessible lavatories.

11.21   The Church has a role in the public domain, scrutinising policies that will affect people throughout life as well as in old age, and being ready to speak and act accordingly.

11.22   The Church is already deeply involved in welfare provision. With the changing role of the voluntary sector in the next decade there will probably be many opportunities for more involvement if churches wish it. We hope that churches which are approached to run projects (or planning to do so on their own initiative) will look critically at what is involved before deciding how to respond.

11.23   The Church has responsibility for its clergy and lay workers. This includes helping clergy and lay workers to confront changes in their working lives and careers as well as to prepare for retirement.

The Contribution of Faith

11.24   This report has affirmed the unique worth and contribution of all people, whatever their age. It celebrates the potential in all created life.

11.25 It has emphasised transition and growth in life, while attempting also to be honest about the loss and difficulties which can be so painfully present in the experience of ageing.

11.26 It has harnessed personal experience and has tried to show the connections between ageing as it is experienced, the observations of the Old and New Testaments, and the achievements of the human sciences.

11.27 The report therefore challenges the negative attitudes to ageing that are widespread in industrialised societies. We have recognised throughout our work that in general people regret the process of ageing. They may associate it with retirement and a loss of status, with declining energy or illness, and perhaps with ugliness, more certainly with loneliness. This reflects the value placed in our society on youth and vitality. At the root of these negative attitudes (often called ageism) seem to be two impulses: a fear of dying and of death, and an ideology which falsely equates success with productivity. Cultures which place high value on economic activity, and individual productivity and consumption tend to have great difficulty in viewing the ageing process positively.

11.28 Christian scripture and tradition call into question the ideologies of both dependence and independence. They take the processes of change and ageing seriously and affirm them as part of God's purpose for us. Christians should be among those who recognise that growing dependence on others can bring out gifts and discoveries and is not necessarily to be feared. Our faith enables us to value the experience, and the maturity of judgement that can come with growing older, and with having time to think, to be thankful and to dream. At the same time faith offers support and succour in coping with the experiences of debilitating disease which may accompany the approach of death. Christians have no easy answers to the questions raised by ageing, but we share confidence about God's love and purpose for the world, along with a sure hope of eternal life.

WARNING

When I am an old woman I shall wear purple
With a red hat which doesn't go, and doesn't suit me.
And I shall spend my pension on brandy and summer gloves
And satin sandals, and say we've no money for butter.
I shall sit down on the pavement when I am tired
And gobble up samples in shops and press alarm bells
And run my stick along the public railings
And make up for the sobriety of my youth.
I shall go out in my slippers in the rain
And pick the flowers in other people's gardens
And learn to spit.

You can wear terrible shirts and grow more fat
And eat three pounds of sausages at a go or only bread and pickle
    for a week
And hoard pens and pencils and beermats and things in boxes.

But now we must have clothes that keep us dry
And pay the rent and not swear in the street
And set a good example for the children.
We must have friends to dinner and read the papers.

But maybe I ought to practise a little now?
So people who know me are not too shocked and surprised
When suddenly I am old and start to wear purple.

Jenny Joseph, *The Faber Book of 20th Century Women's Poems and Plays*. Faber & Faber Ltd, 1987.

REFERENCES

CHAPTER 1

1 Letter from Arthur Creber.
2 *The Economist.* October 26, 1985.
3 Letter from Arthur Creber.
4 Letter from Susan Sawtell.
5 The Reports and Government White Papers relevant for these pieces of legislation are:
   Reform of Social Security   HMSO, 1985.
   Community Care: An Agenda for Action   HMSO, 1988.
   Working for Patients   HMSO, 1989.
   Caring for People   HMSO, 1989.
6 *Faith in the City.* CHP, 1985.
   Not Just for the Poor. CHP, 1986.
   No Mean City. Methodist Division for Social Responsibility, 1989.
   Living Faith in the City. CHP, 1990.
7 *Not Just for the Poor.* Op. cit.
8 Philip Toynbee. *End of a Journey.* Bloomsbury, 1988.
9 Philip Larkin. *Collected Poems.* Faber & Faber, 1988.
10 Ronald Blythe. *The View in Winter.* Allen Lane, 1979.
11 Further details are available from the General Synod Board for Social Responsibility, Church House, Great Smith Street, London SW1P 3NZ.
12 Thirty years is the customary span for demographic projections.

CHAPTER 2

1 Table 1.8 *Social Trends 20.* HMSO, 1990.
2 Table A.2 *Social Trends 20.* HMSO, 1990.
3 Table 7.2 *Social Trends 20.* HMSO, 1990.
4 Table 3.5 *Informal Carers.* HMSO, 1988.
5 Table 6 *Population Trends* (Winter 88). HMSO, 1988.
6 Tables 2, 3 *Census 1981. Country of Birth: Great Britain.* HMSO, 1981.
7 Table 12.4 *General Household Survey.* HMSO, 1986.
8 Malcolm Wicks and Melanie Henwood, 'The Demographic and Social Circumstances of Elderly People' in *Mental Health Problems in Old Age.* Eds. Brian Gearing, Malcolm Johnson and Tom Heller. Open University, 1988.

9 Malcolm Johnson. 'The Meaning of Old Age' in S. Redfern *Nursing Elderly People*. Churchill Livingstone, 1986.
10 *An Ageing Population*. Family Policy Studies Centre, 1988.
11 Ibid.
12 Table 12c *General Household Survey*. HMSO, 1986.
13 Table 1.19 *Social Trends 20*. HMSO, 1990.

CHAPTER 3

1 James Fowler. *Becoming Adult, Becoming Christian: Adult Development and Christian Faith*. Harper and Row, 1985.
2 T. S. Eliot. *Four Quartets* (Burnt Norton). Faber & Faber, 1936.
3 2 Samuel 19:31-40.

CHAPTER 4

1 William H. Vanstone. *The Stature of Waiting*. Darton Longman & Todd, 1982.

CHAPTER 5

1 Carl Jung. *Memories, Dreams, Reflections*. Flamingo (Harper Collins), 1983.
2 James Fowler. Op. cit.
3 Walter Brueggemann. *Hope Within History*. John Knox Press, Atlanta USA, 1987.
4 See for example Jacqueline Line's 'Dementia—a theological reflection'. *Quarterly Journal of the Christian Council on Ageing*. Summer, 1988.

CHAPTER 6

1 Annie Franklin & Bob Franklin. 'Age and Power' in *Youth, Inequality and Society*. Eds. Jeffs and Smith. Macmillan, 1990.
2 Ibid.
3 Op. cit.
4 Ibid.
5 J. Dillon. *Against Ageism*. Search Project, Newcastle, ND.
6 Anthea Tinker. *Why the Sudden Interest in Ageing?* King's College, London, 1990.
7 Donald Winnicott. *Playing and Reality*. Penguin, 1974.
8 Alison Norman. 'Mental disorder and elderly members of ethnic minority groups' in *Mental Health Problems in Old Age*. Eds. Brian Gearing, Malcolm Johnson and Tom Heller. Open University, 1988.

9 Ibid.
10 Alison Norman. Op. cit.
11 Ibid.
12 *Ethnic Minority Senior Citizens—the Question of Policy.* Standing Conference of Ethnic Minority Senior Citizens, 1986.
13 Alison Norman. *Rights and Risks.* Centre for Policy on Ageing, 1980.

CHAPTER 7

1 Letter from Anthony Dyson.
2 Matthew Arnold. *The Scholar Gipsy.* J. M. Dent and Sons Ltd, 1965 (first published 1903).
3 *Euthanasia.* British Medical Association, 1988.
4 Eric Midwinter. *Age is Opportunity: Education and Older People.* Centre for Policy on Ageing, 1982.
5 Frank E. Moss and Val J. Halamandaris. *Too old, too sick, too bad: Nursing Homes in America.* Aspen Systems Corporation, Maryland, 1977.
6 Ann Morisy. *Rapport with an Inner Voice: the contribution of Adult Education and the Christian Tradition to Healthy Ageing.* Unpublished dissertation, 1987.
7 Jean Martin and Ceridwen Roberts. *Women in Employment: A Lifetime Perspective.* HMSO, 1984.
8 Press Release. The Volunteer Centre. May, 1990.
9 *Involve* Bulletin No 52/7. The Volunteer Centre, 1986.
10 Alan Walker. 'The Politics of Ageing in Britain' in *Dependency and Independency in Old Age: Theoretical perspectives and policy alternatives.* Eds. Chris Phillipson, Miriam Bernard and Patricia Strang. Croom Helm, 1986.
11 'Questions of growing grey in prosperity'. *The Guardian,* 27 March, 1990.
12 Jeremy Laurance. *New Society.* 18 March, 1988.

CHAPTER 8

1 In Peter Townsend. *The Last Refuge.* Routledge & Kegan Paul, 1964.
2 *Health and Welfare: The Development of Community Care.* Ministry of Health, 1963.
3 *Public Expenditure: The Social Services,* Vol. 2 (HC 702) HMSO, 1980.
4 *Growing Older.* (Cmnd 8173). HMSO, 1981.
5 *The Experience of Caring for Elderly and Handicapped Dependants.* Equal Opportunities Commission, 1980.
6 Hazel Green. *Informal Carers: A Survey carried out on behalf of the Department of Health and Social Services as part of the General Household Survey 1985.* HMSO, 1988.

7 In Muriel Nissel and Lucy Bonnerjea. *Family Care of the Handicapped: Who Pays?* Policy Studies Institute, 1982.
8 Graham Fennell, Chris Phillipson and Clare Wenger. 'The Process of Ageing: Social Aspects' in *Elderly People in the Community: their Service Needs.* DHSS, 1983.
9 Hazel Green. Op. cit.
10 Anna Briggs. *Who Cares?* Association of Carers, 1983.
11 Hazel Green. Op. cit.
12 Anna Briggs. Op. cit.
13 Muriel Nissel and Lucy Bonnerjea. Op. cit.
14 *Family Policy 6.* Winter, 1989.
15 Fay Wright. 'Single Carers: Employment, Housework and Caring' in *Labour of Love.* Eds. Janet Finch and Dulcie Groves. Routledge & Kegan Paul, 1983.
16 Equal Opportunities Commission. Op. cit.
17 In Jill Pitkeathley. *It's My Duty Isn't It?* Souvenir, 1989.
18 Ibid.
19 In Judith Oliver. 'The Caring Wife' in Judith Finch and Dulcie Groves. Op. cit.
20 Ibid.
21 *Community Care: An Agenda for Action.* HMSO, 1988.
   Managing Social Services for the Elderly More Effectively. Audit Commission, 1985.
   Making a Reality of Community Care. Audit Commission, 1986.
22 Audit Commission, 1986. Op. cit.
23 Anna Briggs. Op. cit.
24 Fay Wright. Op. cit.
25 Anne Borrowdale. *A Woman's Work: Changing Christian Attitudes.* SPCK, 1989.
26 Virginia Woolf. *Women and Writing.* Women's Press, 1979.
27 Isobel Allen. 'The Elderly and their Informal Carers' in *The Elderly in the Community: their Service Needs.* DHSS, 1982.
28 William Alwyn Lishman. 'An acquired global impairment of intellect, memory and personality, but without impairment of consciousness', *Organic Psychiatry.* Blackwell, 1978.
29 *Organic Mental Impairment in the Elderly.* Royal College of Physicians Committee on Geriatrics, 1981.
30 D. W. K. Kay, P. Beamish, and M. Roth. *Old Age Mental Disorders in Newcastle upon Tyne.* British Journal of Psychiatry (1964) 110. D. W. K. Kay, K. Bergmann, E. M. Foster, R. A. McKechnie and M. Roth, *Mental Illness and Hospital Usage in the Elderly: a random sample followed up.* Comprehensive Psychiatry (1970) 11.
31 W. T. Thom. 'Housing Policies' in *The provision of care for the elderly.* Eds. John Kinnaird, John Brotherston and James Williams. Churchill, 1981.

32 Chris Gilleard. *Living with Dementia: Community Care of the Mentally Infirm.* Croom Helm, 1984.
33 A. Charlesworth and D. Wilkins. *Dependency among old people in geriatric wards, psycho-geriatric wards and residential homes 1977-1981.* University Hospital of South Manchester (1982) Research Report 6.
34 D. W. K. Kay et al. 1964. Op. cit.
35 D. W. K. Kay et al. 1970. Op. cit.
36 Chris Gilleard. Op. cit.
37 Valerie Goldberg. *Voluntary support for the elderly mentally confused people in the community.* Surrey Council for Mental Health, 1988.
38 Royal College of Physicians. Op. cit.
39 Nancy Mace, Peter Rabins, with B. A. Castleton, C. Cloke and E. McEwen. *The 36 Hour Day: Caring at home for confused elderly people.* Hodder & Stoughton/Age Concern, 1985. Elaine Murphy. *Dementia and Mental Illness in the Old.* Papermac, 1986.
40 Royal College of Physicians. Op. cit.
41 Hugo Petszch. *Does he know how frightening he is in his strangeness? A study in Attitudes to Dementing People.* University of Edinburgh Department of Christian Ethics and Practical Theology Occasional Paper, 1984.
42 Harry Williams. *Some Day I'll find You.* Mitchell Beazley, 1982.
43 Una Kroll. *Growing Older.* Collins Fount, 1988.
44 Judith Oliver in *Caring for the Elderly and Handicapped: Community Care Policies and Women's Lives.* Equal Opportunities Commission, 1982.
45 Chris Gilleard. Op. cit.
46 Elizabeth Forsythe. *Alzheimer's Disease: The Long Bereavement.* Faber & Faber, 1990.
47 Joseph Fletcher. *Humanhood: Essays in Bio-medical Ethics.* Prometheus, 1979.
48 Interestingly even William Vanstone (op. cit), who has done much to help us to grasp that we are as much in God's image in being as in doing, cannot bring himself to see in the schizophrenic person someone who is 'waiting'.
49 Hugo Petzsch. Op. cit.
50 Robert Wennberg. *Life in the balance: exploring the abortion controversy.* Eedermans, 1985.
51 Alexine Crawford. *Christian.* 14 July/Aug, 1989.
52 Hugo Petzsch, 1984. Op. cit.
53 Glenn D. Weaver. 'Senile Dementia and a Resurrection Theology'. *Theology Today.* Vol. XLII. No. 4, 1986.

CHAPTER 9

1 Table 7.26 *Social Trends 20.* HMSO, 1990.
2 Table 7.25 *Social Trends 20.* HMSO, 1990.
3 *The Times.* 28 November, 1989.

4 Press Release. Department of Social Security. 20 February, 1990.
5 Table 5.4 *Social Trends.* HMSO, 1990.
6 'Questions of growing grey in prosperity'. *The Guardian,* 27 March, 1990.
7 *Economic Trends.* December, 1988.
8 Ibid.
9 Ibid.
10 House of Commons *Hansard.* 11 May, 1989.
11 Press Release Department of Social Security. Op. cit.
12 House of Commons *Hansard.* 31 March, 1988.
13 *Reform of Social Security.* HMSO, 1985.
14 House of Commons *Hansard.* 14 December, 1988.
15 *The Discretionary Social Fund—Its Impact on Older People.* Age Concern, May 1989.
16 *An Ageing Population.* Family Policy Studies Centre Factsheet No. 2. July, 1988.
17 Anthea Tinker. *Staying at Home: Helping Elderly People.* Department of the Environment, 1984.
18 Anthea Tinker. *An Evaluation of Very Sheltered Housing.* HMSO, 1989.
19 Op. cit.
20 *Income Support Limits for Residential Care and Nursing Homes.* Age Concern, August, 1989.
21 Roy Parker. Quoted in *A Positive Choice.* HMSO, 1988.
22 *A Positive Choice.* Ibid.
23 Eric Midwinter. *Age is Opportunity: Education and Older People.* Centre for Policy on Ageing, 1982.
24 Ibid.

CHAPTER 10

1 *Children in the Way.* NS/CHP, 1988.
  Leaves on the Tree. NS/CHP, 1990.
2 Letter from the Revd Elizabeth Capper and Frank Quickenden.
3 Letter from Dorothy Seaward.
4 Letter from Susan Sawtell.
5 Bishop Jim Thompson. *Thought for the Day.* 6 July, 1989.
6 Letter from Arthur Creber.
7 Unpublished paper on evangelism with elderly people, prepared by the Church Army.
8 Maggie Kuhn. Quoted in *Christian Theology and Ageing: A Basic Affirmation.* Ed. William B. Clements. Harper & Row, New York, 1981.

APPENDIX A

Principles of Residential Care

People who move into a residential establishment should do so by positive choice. A distinction should be made between need for accommodation and need for services. No one should be required to change their permanent accommodation in order to receive services which could be made available to them in their own homes.

Living in a residential establishment should be a positive experience ensuring a better quality of life than the resident could enjoy in any other setting.

Local authorities should make efforts, as a matter of urgency, to meet the special needs of people from ethnic minority communities for residential and other services.

Every person who moves into a residential establishment should continue to have access to the full range of community support services.

Residents should have access to leisure, educational and other facilities offered by the local community and the right to invite and receive relatives and friends as they choose.

Residential staff are the major resource and should be valued as such. The importance of their contribution needs to be recognised and enhanced.

Reproduced with permission from *A Positive Choice*. HMSO, 1988.

APPENDIX B

James Fowler's Stages of Faith

(Primal Faith, sometimes included by Fowler as Stage 1)

1 Intuitive Projective Faith
2 Mythic-Literal Faith
3 Synthetic-Conventional Faith
4 Individuative-Reflective Faith
5 Paradoxical-Consolidative Faith (now called Conjunctive Faith by Fowler)
6 Universalising Faith

The child moves from the dependence and trust on parents as superordinate power and wisdom (primal faith) to the wider experience of sharing in stories, symbols and rituals. These enrich his understanding and provide powerful identification and aspiration, guidance and reassurance as he endeavours to understand the world and give it unity and sense (Stage 1—intuitive-projective faith). From this she or he moves to rely on stories, rules and the implicit values of the family's faith experience. Stories, practices and the family's beliefs are valued but in a concrete and literal sense. She or he is secure in this, but unable to find an overall direction and meaning from the component parts (Stage 2—mythical-literal faith). Next he or she moves to search for 'a story of my stories', a sense of the meaning of life generally, and of meaning and purpose in his or her own life in particular. The elements which make up this personal and original faith system is compiled of conventional elements, to be subjected to self-critical reflection and enquiry (Stage 3—synthetic conventional faith). Later the person moves to Stage 4 (individuative-reflective faith) which is more personally chosen and believed, with an awareness that his or her views are different from that of some other people, and able to be expressed in abstract terms. In Stage 5 (paradoxical—consolidative) many different ideas and perspectives, suppressed or evaded before, are worked at, contradictions and tensions held in balance and apparently simple propositional statements reached. Stage 6 (universalising) is the final stage, typical of saints, where coherence gives a new simplicity centred on 'a oneness beyond but inclusive of the manyness of Being'.

Reproduced from *Children in the Way* pages 52 and 53. NS/CHP, 1988.

FURTHER READING AND RESOURCES

Growing Older. Una Kroll. Fount, 1988.

The View in Winter. Reflections on Old Age. Ronald Blythe. Allen Lane, 1979.

Aspects of Ageing. Alison Norman. Centre for Policy on Ageing, 1986.

Letting Go: Caring for the Dying and Bereaved. Ian Ainsworth-Smith & Peter Speck. SPCK, 1982.

Ageing, the Fulfilment of life. Henri Nouwen & W. Gaffney. Image Books, 1966.

Towards a Practical Theology of Ageing. Brynolf Lyon. Fortress Press, 1985.

A Year Lost and Found. Michael Mayne. DLT, 1987.

The Ageing Population—Burden or Challenge? Nicholas Wells & Charles Freer. Macmillan, 1988.

Good Retirement Guide. Rosemary Brown. Bloomsbury. Published annually.

From Generation to Generation. Julia Burton-Jones. Jubilee Centre (Cambridge) Research Paper No. 9. 1990.

Carers: Out of Sight, Out of Mind. A Jubilee Centre (Cambridge) Video. 1990.

Serving Carers: A Handbook for you and your church. Jubilee Centre (Cambridge). 1990.

It's My Duty Isn't It? Jill Pitkeathley. Souvenir, 1989.

Life Later On: Older People in the Church. Ann Webber. Triangle Press, 1990.

Age Concern produces useful information sheets and a wide range of publications. The following may be of particular interest:

Living, Loving and Ageing: Sexual and Personal Relationships in later life. Wendy Greengross and Sally Greengross. 1989.

Your Rights. 1989-90. Sally West.

Coming of Age: A positive guide to growing old. Consultant Editor David Hobman.

Housing Options for Older People. David Bookbinder.

ORGANISATIONS CONCERNED WITH AGEING

Christian Council on Ageing
(CCOA)
The Old Court
Greens Norton
Nr Towcester
Northants NN12 8BS
Tel: (0327) 50481

Research into Ageing
40 Queen Victoria Street
London EC4N 4SA
Tel: 071-236 4365

Centre for Policy on Ageing
25-31 Ironmonger Row
London EC1V 3QP
Tel: 071-253 1787

Age Concern England
(National Old People's Welfare
Council)
60 Pitcairn Road
Mitcham
Surrey CR4 3LL
Tel: 081-679 8000

Age Concern Institute of
Gerontology
Cornwall House Annexe
Waterloo
London SE1 8TX
Tel: 071-872 3035

Alzheimer's Disease Society
158/160 Balham High Road
London SW12 9BN
Tel: 081-675 6557/8/9/0

Help the Aged
16-18 St James's Walk
London EC1R 0BE
Tel: 071-253 0253

Family Policy Studies Centre
231 Baker Street
London NW1 6XE
Tel: 071-486 8211/2

Policy Studies Institute
100 Park Village East
London NW1
Tel: 071-387 2171

Carers' National Association
29 Chilworth Mews
London W2 3RG
Tel: 071-724 7776

Grandparents Federation
78 Cook's Spinney
Harlow
Essex CM20 3BL
Tel: (0279) 37145

RSVP (Retired & Senior Volunteer
Programme)
c/o CSV
237 Pentonville Road
London N1 9NJ
Tel: 071-278 6601